SEMIOTEXT(E) INTERVENTION SERIES

Published by Semiotext(e)
PO Box 629, South Pasadena, CA 91031
www.semiotexte.com

Design: Hedi El Kholti

ISBN: 978-1-63590-276-1

10 9 8 7 6 5 4 3 2 1

Distributed by the MIT Press, Cambridge, MA
and London, England
Printed in the United States of America

Franco "Bifo" Berardi

Thinking Gaza

An Essay on Ferocity

semiotext(e)
intervention
series ◻ 39

Contents

Tyger Tyger, burning bright,
In the forests of the night;
What immortal hand or eye,
Could frame thy fearful symmetry?

In what distant deeps or skies.
Burnt the fire of thine eyes?
On what wings dare he aspire?
What the hand, dare seize the fire?

And what shoulder, & what art,
Could twist the sinews of thy heart?
And when thy heart began to beat.
What dread hand? & what dread feet?

What the hammer? what the chain,
In what furnace was thy brain?
What the anvil? what dread grasp.
Dare its deadly terrors clasp?

When the stars threw down their spears,
And water'd heaven with their tears:
Did he smile his work to see?
Did he who made the Lamb make thee?

Tyger Tyger burning bright,
In the forests of the night:
What immortal hand or eye,
Dare frame thy fearful symmetry?
—William Blake, "The Tyger"

> Auschwitz demonstrated irrefutably that culture has failed. … All post-Auschwitz culture, including its urgent critique, is garbage.
> —Theodor W. Adorno, *Negative Dialectics*

In the present irremediable defeat of humanity, the task of the thinker is simply to tell the truth.

Truth, however, is too demanding a word, so it is better to say instead: The task of the thinker is to say what drama takes place in the theater of his awareness.

Let's call this drama "truth."

In the past, when it was possible to have even a little hope, it was sometimes necessary and forgivable to hide something of the truth, waiting for better times.

Now we know that there will be no better times, and we know that there is no longer any hope. Now we know that the human is retreating into inaccessible places of desertion, while inhuman horror advances and the automaton takes over the command functions.

We are therefore left alone with the despair and impotence of the truth: the definitive, final, and completely useless truth.

It is necessary to share this truth.

Thinking, now, is definitively irrelevant, except for those who think.

And those who think are not alone. Those one who think are befriended by accomplices who are contemplating the same drama.

What is happening now—genocide erected as the new rule of history, the unleashing of aggressive dementia in every facet of social relations—is much worse than what happened in Germany in 1933, because now it is definitive and unchallenged, and because in the future there will be no Stalingrad.

This is why thinking is terrible, but indispensable.

Because there is no other cure, there is no other way, to preserve the only thing that remains: self-respect.

1

FEROCITY

Whether humankind can survive the combined onslaught of climate change, rampant aggressive dementia, and destructive artificial intelligence technologies is currently uncertain.

It is certain, however, that civilization —the progressive "humanization" of the human, the predominance of language over the natural ferocity of instinct—is disintegrating.

We have long perceived the signs of this disintegration; we have long seen that liberal deregulation has been paving the way for the prevalence of force in relationships between human animals.

Now the collapse is underway, after the atrocious aggression unleashed by Hamas on October 7, 2023—an aggression that must be defined as a pogrom, similar to those that the Jewish people have suffered over the centuries in many European countries, and similar to those that the Palestinians of the West Bank have suffered for years at the hands of armed gangs of Israeli settlers.

In the year of uninterrupted atrocity that followed, the failure of the project called "civilization" became evident, and ferocity regained the upper hand: the return of the beast in human history, the return of homicidal violence as a primordial reflex of self-defense and survival.

The name Gaza appears for the first time in the military documents of Pharaoh Thutmose III in the fifteenth century BC.

In Semitic languages, the city's name means "fierce."

Throughout history, men have often given themselves high-sounding titles, exhibited aggressive postures, and threatened disasters; similarly, the Gazawi called themselves "ferocious."

The unhappiness of the world depends to some extent on this self-identification with greatness and ferocity, with a power that we do not have but that we like to flaunt and that we are sometimes forced to flaunt in the hope of frightening others who are, in reality, more ferocious than us.

That sandy strip of land overlooking the eastern Mediterranean is mentioned many times in the Bible, and in ancient Egyptian documents and inscriptions of Ramesses II, Thutmose III, and Seti I.

When the Israelites arrived in the Promised Land, Gaza was a Philistine city, and among its inhabitants were the Anakim, a population that was dwelling in the mountainous regions of Canaan and some coastal areas.

It was in Gaza that Samson, blinded and in chains, caused the temple dedicated to the worship of Dagon, where over three thousand people could gather, to collapse. He himself died, taking to hell thousands of Philistines.

After October 7, 2023, the Israelis reacted with cruelty and ferocity.

If cruelty is a perverse desire of humans, ferocity is an animal reflex inscribed in the instinct of self-preservation.

The beginning of the extinction of so-called civilization is marked by this return of ferocity as the sole regulator of exchanges between humans.

At least in recent centuries, civilization has been essentially the attempt to submit ferocity to politics and instinct to will, which can together be summarized as the submission of chaos to language.

After Gaza, it is time to recognize that this attempt to humanize history has failed, and that there will not be a second try.

It is time to recognize that the experiment called "civilization" has failed. What is left of civilization is the destructive power of technology—particularly, military technology. When ferocity prevails, technology becomes a function of war.

We are left now with our ability to kill in a much more sophisticated and systematic way than any other ferocious animal.

"Thinking Gaza" means first of all recognizing the irremediable failure of the universalism of reason and democracy—that is, the dissolution of the very core of civilization.

But it also means looking for escape routes from the future that awaits us, and that awaits those who have been born in this century that promises to be the last.

To those who were conceived in the dark light of this final century, we owe this last act of thought, so that they can desert history, along paths that we cannot yet imagine.

"Thinking Gaza" implies the acknowledgment that words mean the opposite of what they are supposed to mean according to history, psychology, and semiotics.

In the age of ferocity, language is only useful to lie, to cheat, to subjugate, and to exploit.

In current discourse, in hyperaccelerated media, there is no time for critical analysis, there is no time for ethical discrimination. There is no time to listen and to understand.

Techno-media temporality is contracted to such an extreme that understanding and critical elaboration are impossible. This implies that human history is over, because the human (beyond any speciesist privilege) is the sphere where words have meaning, and can be interpreted, so that language can mediate the relations between bodies. Ever since language became another battlefield where the most powerful imposes his own interpretation, ever since the paths of criticism and independent thought were cut off in the name of speed, we have entered the realm of ferocity.

In the realm of ferocity, every form of language becomes a tool for extermination.

The law was intended as universal frame for regulating the relationships between the actors of the social game, who were considered subjects of language.

In recent centuries, the law has established itself as a universal discourse, alternative to the ferocity of tribal belonging.

The modern assertion of the universality of reason was made possible by the Jewish intellectual tradition: by the contributions of those who were allowed to think in a nomadic place, in a place that was not a place of belonging.

Even the internationalist idea, supported by communist workers, has been made thinkable thanks to the contribution of Jewish culture, which was free from ethnic or territorial belonging.

This is why the tragedy of Gaza seems definitive and irremediable: because a state and an army that pretend to be the expression of that culture, as the heirs of that history, have betrayed the Jewish intellectual contribution to modern civilization.

"Thinking Gaza" means acknowledging the betrayal of Jewish culture by the Zionist leadership and by the vast majority of the Israeli people.

The failure of universal reason and the betrayal of modern Jewish culture are two sides of the same coin.

From its start, the State of Israel has betrayed and denied the Jewish intellectual tradition; but today, after Gaza, this disdainful negation of the very illusion of the universality of human reason has become Israel's political program and common sense.

The military action of the Israel Defense Forces and the complicity of the Israeli people with the genocide unleashed by Netanyahu's government irreversibly mark a regression toward particularism and the cancellation of any hope of a "human" future.

This is the lesson that Israel has given us: in the sphere of history, the victims do not know how to and cannot ask for peace or reparations but can only seek revenge. This means that today's victims will never be anything other than victims, unless they manage to transform themselves into exterminators.

After the Israeli genocide, law, universalism, and democracy appear as illusions that predators have used to maintain their power over their prey. But now these illusions have dissolved, and what is revealed is the ferocious face of colonialism, of which Israel is the latest manifestation.

The fight against Nazism and the victory against Hitler's Germany appeared as a reassertion of the principles of modern universalism.

The Nazis' ferocity was defeated by the symmetrical ferocity of the antifascist powers, but beyond the ferocity of the Second World War, a time of peace, of law, of democracy seemed poised to emerge and to last forever.

This was the meaning of *Nie wieder*: "Never again." Those words were at the foundation of the cultural and political education of the generation that grew up after the end of the Second World War—my generation.

Looking back today, I feel that this belief was an illusion.

"Never again" was temporary, because the foundations of a society capable of expelling ferocity from the sphere of human civilization had not been laid.

Those foundations are fraternity and social equality. It was only the organized force of the working class that had made such a condition possible, but the source of ferocity (exploitation, transformation of life time into exchange value) was never eliminated. The genocide that Israel has committed in revenge against Hamas makes clear that *Nie wieder* was a lie. The heirs of the victims of the Nazi genocide were preparing to become strong enough to perpetrate their own genocide.

Trauma

The traumatic violence that was suffered during the years of the Shoah could only have devastating effects.

The most devastating effect was the birth of the colonialist and hyperarmed Zionist state, which is the proof that universalism has no truth in the face of history, and that nationalism is the only way to protect one's existence.

The aggressive reterritorialization of the survivors of the Holocaust is the consequence of a trauma that evidently has not been processed, probably because there are traumas that cannot be processed.

The Zionist state presents itself as a way to prevent the possible recurrence of anti-Semitic aggression, but it is also a vengeful processing of trauma—and these two things cannot be distinguished, cannot be separated.

If the only way to avoid the repetition of genocide is to build a state destined to perpetrate genocide, this implies that ferocity, in history, has taken the place of law.

This is why the Holocaust has left a definitive mark in the history of Europe and the world: because it demonstrates that reason must bow its head in the face of ferocity. And that only ferocity can protect against ferocity.

Zionist reterritorialization, aggressive as any reterritorialization, was rational because it served a rational purpose: since universal reason had not protected the Jews from Nazism and extermination, some of the Jewish survivors allowed themselves to think that the only way to escape further aggressions was to equip themselves with tools for self-protection. They decided to do whatever it took in order not to be prey again, even if this entailed turning into predators. This is the rationality of ferocity, which cannot coexist with the universality of reason.

Israeli reterritorialization has demonstrated that there is no possibility of processing the traumas of history, because the only way to emancipate oneself from oppression is through revenge, and because the only way to avoid extermination is to exterminate.

In the specific case of Israel, revenge had an asymmetrical character: it was not carried out against the Germans, nor against the Europeans, responsible for the genocide of the 1940s. Instead, it was carried out against a population that could not defend itself and that had nothing to do with the anti-Semitic injustice.

This happens sometimes: those who suffered violence because they did not have enough strength to rebel exercise their revenge against someone who is weaker than them.

Over the decades, Israel has evolved in the direction of accentuating its exclusive and fundamentalist character: in 2018, violating a fundamental principle of modern political universalism, the Knesset decided that the State of Israel is the state of the Jews, the same way the Iranian Republic is the state of the Muslims.

The meaning of the Knesset's decision was clear from the moment it was made, but only in 2023 were we able to understand what consequences this evolution entails, not only for Israel, not only for the Middle East, but for the entire world.

The Second World War was an immense tragedy, but it did not erase the possibility of believing in a better future. In fact, the liberation from the Nazi fascists sparked a fresh energy that inspired the majority of the world.

In 1945, the democratic promise sounded credible, and the motto "never again" was persuasive, because despite what had just happened, a future of equality, solidarity, and democracy seemed to be at hand.

A movement then began that for the next thirty years allowed a predominantly young population to participate in a project, which did not seem utopian, founded on equality and peace.

But today, it is different: What is left of the hope and the energy that allowed us to emerge from the horror of war?

Nothing is left of that optimism, and nothing remains of that energy. Those young people have senesced both demographically and intellectually. Now old, they retreat in fear and resentment, unable to face the enormity of the threats: war is back, extermination seems to be the regulator of relations between the colonialist Global North and the migrant masses fleeing the Global South, of which the Palestinians have become the bloody symbol.

This is why nothing is left of that optimism: equality has been cancelled, criminalized, disparaged as a disvalue, as a danger to the fate of the competitive economy. Solidarity is impossible because of the precariousness of labor. Peace is a utopia due to the predominance of nationalism, a political cancer that replaces solidarity among workers and affection among erotic bodies with camaraderie among young men who prepare to fight.

Democracy has been ridiculed by the domination of financial automatisms and forgotten because of the return of war.

Who can believe in a future that is not fatal?

Who can trust the promises of power?

In the face of the power of weapons, the only thing you can do is bow your head, obey, and suffer. No promise to hear, no promise to keep.

The common ground of the Zionist community is political nationalism and fanatic fundamentalism: the only effective law is the law of the strongest, the law of the superior race. The law of the God who proclaims to be the Lord of the Armies. A racist god that gave life to white supremacy.

"Thinking Gaza" means to think no future, no hope, no universality, no humanity.

The abyss is wide open and we cannot help but see it.

We must gaze into the abyss, we must gauge the breadth and the depth of the abyss.

We must draw a map of the abyss, while precipitously falling into it.

Understanding Desertion

History is losing the humanistic horizon that was the promise of modernity, while thought, having lost all political power, is forced to retreat in horror, transformed into a helpless contemplation of progressive dehumanization.

Barbarism is the condition in which the word is not capable of being understood, nor shared.

When the word can no longer be shared, then the law is no longer made of words but only of nature: only the law of the strongest applies, only the law of the predator operates. Barbarism, in this sense, is ferocity.

When we enter the era in which the relationships among humans are no longer mediated by language but by ferocity, then evolution regains the upper hand over history, and natural selection takes the lead without the mediation of law.

The dimension of history is left behind, and we fully reenter the sphere of nature. The only legacy of historical times is technology, which multiplies the strength of the predator.

The subject of thought can only be its own impotence.

This is why the martyrdom of Gaza, beyond being a tragedy that has overwhelmed the lives of millions of people (and above all, children), is evidence of the passage into an era in which there will never be justice nor peace.

Expecting justice and peace in a possible future just means having not understood.

Those who continue to act as if it were possible to restore the universality of reason are not understanding.

Those who believe that political will can reverse the irreversible are not understanding.

Those who believe in the effectiveness of politics are not understanding.

Those who think that the word *democracy* has some meaning are not understanding.

But we must understand, because this is the only thing we have left: understanding.

We have been left with the disenchanted vision of a world in which domination belongs to the ferocity of the survival instinct and the ferocity of extermination technology.

We must have the courage to understand that there will be no return to democracy, and no end to war, and no limit to the expansion of inhumanity.

We need to understand because only after understanding can we begin to take the only reasonable action: moving away from the historical bond, separating ourselves from the human consortium, forgetting identity(ies), and therefore discovering—or rather, establishing—a nonhistorical, nonpolitical dimension, in which friendship, joy, and courtesy are possible.

Those who understand, desert; they abandon any attempt to interact with the historical process, because history has revealed itself as unstoppable catastrophe.

Those who have the courage to understand will not contribute to reproducing the human race, because the human experiment has failed, and this time the failure is without appeal.

We Will Live

On March 8, 2024, in many cities of the world, feminist demonstrations were full of Palestinian flags.

This did not mean that women support Hamas or Hezbollah, or the Islamist fanatics in general. Nor did it mean that women accept the patriarchal violence of Islamic culture.

Those flags carried a very clear message: We are on the side of the women and children who have been suffering from the systematic oppression of the Zionist state for seventy-five years, and who at this moment are dying by the thousands under the bombs of the Israeli Air Force.

On that day in Paris, women's demonstrations were attacked by groups belonging to a Zionist organization called Nous vivrons.

I had never heard of this organization, and my attention was drawn precisely by their name, by the way they had chosen to identify themselves: "We will live."

On October 7, a pogrom occurred. It was not the first pogrom of the twenty-first century, as some have said. There had been others before it: the pogroms against the Rohingya population in Myanmar, the pogrom that the Islamists of Daesh carried out against the Yazidi people, and also the pogroms that the Israeli settlers conducted in the occupied territories of the West Bank on several occasions.

After October 7, it was completely understandable that Jews felt the danger of anti-Semitism reemerging. The trauma of the Holocaust resurfaced, provoking an understandable, and even shareable, reaction of self-defense.

The reaction of those who are the object of an attack against their life and that of their community is an animal reflex of self-defense and survival. A *ferocious* reaction, in the etymological sense of the word.

We want to live, we will live, we don't care about others.

May others suffer the pains of hell, may others die with their families. Let a genocide happen, as long as we can survive.

A ferocious reaction—as natural as the survival instinct—knows neither law nor history, it knows not the concatenation of causes and effects, of rights and wrongs. It knows only fear and the immediate movement of the hands protecting the head, of the legs escaping imminent danger.

The expression *Nous vivrons* horrifies me, but I understand it perfectly.

Those who say "we will live no matter what" are not interested in understanding that the Zionist state has been killing, humiliating, destroying, oppressing Palestinians for seventy-five years.

They don't want to know anything, because inherited trauma has blinded them to the suffering of others.

The first two decades of the twenty-first century had already shown the return of a climate of unquenchable hatred and nationalistic aggression in many parts of the world, but only after October 7 were we forced to recognize that ferocity had regained the upper hand over civilization.

Since then, the collective mind has tuned into the wavelength of the inevitability of genocide, of an unstoppable genocidal chain.

What can stop this chain, if the grandchildren of the Holocaust victims have turned into promoters of a new holocaust?

Cruelty and Postmodern Baroque

If ferocity is the logic of animal survival, cruelty is the human desire to inflict pain.

Countless incidents described by journalists and recorded by video cameras show that the violence of Israeli soldiers is not aimed at carrying out a questionable military operation but is aimed at humiliating and ridiculing the victims, at torturing them, at inflicting intolerable pain.

Many photos and videos have appeared on social media in which IDF soldiers disembowel dolls found in houses once inhabited by Palestinian girls, set fire to bookcases found in those homes, and let themselves be filmed while laughing at the terror of a family, or at the pain of a father who has lost his children or of a woman who has lost her entire family.

The atrocities performed by Israeli soldiers surpass the cruelty of those in our memory, those of which our parents had spoken, our parents who witnessed the actions of the Nazi troops on Italian soil, in Marzabotto, in Sant'Anna di Stazzema.

If ferocity is the reemergence of an animality that has certainly not been eliminated by the development of civilization, cruelty suggests that brutality has become a technology aimed at turning into terror everything that used to be useful, or reassuring.

In September 2024, four thousand pagers exploded simultaneously, victimizing thousands and sowing panic throughout Lebanon.

This is the proof of the extraordinary genius of the Israeli Holocaust industry, proof of the technical and economic superiority of the Israeli extermination apparatus.

Similarly, the Nazis were superior in 1939, when they attacked Poland and then France, using a technical advantage that allowed their troops to move more quickly and to quickly occupy territories. But German technical superiority did not last forever, and in the end Anglo-American bombings destroyed German cities, inflicting unspeakable suffering on the military and civilian populations of those cities.

In the competition for ferocity, the Anglo-Americans showed that they were superior to the German Nazis, as demonstrated by the bombings of Hamburg, Dresden, Tokyo, Hiroshima, Nagasaki …

In 2024, we have learned that ferocity and cruelty are endless, and that the chain of revenge cannot be broken.

This year, we have been obliged to acknowledge that the history of civilization is over, and there is no reason to expect that anyone will restore hope.

Israel has forever erased hope from the future of the human race.

On the days of Purim, the salvation of the Jewish people is celebrated: on that day, Esther helped the Jews to escape the extermination prepared by the evil Haman.

On this occasion, the Jews celebrate with four *mitzvot* (precepts), among which, in addition to the public reading of the Megillat Esther, the offering of food to the poor is important.

The Zionists, a caricatured perversion of what the Jews once were, wickedly prefer to starve two million people, and to use hunger as a weapon of war and oppression.

But despite having betrayed everything that was progressive in their culture, the Israelis have not lost the desire to have fun, and are staging an obscene carnival of violence. According to a report in the Italian newsletter *Anbamed*: "Hundreds of Israeli Jewish settlers invaded the Al-Aqsa Mosque for Purim, the Jewish carnival. The occupation forces chased away the Muslim faithful and closed the entry crossings, leaving free entry for the playful antics of the settlers. The Israeli soldiers entered the mosques, trampling on the prayer rugs with their boots."[1]

As I do not believe in any god, I am as indifferent to the sacrilege of these disgraceful Zionist desecrators as to the sacrilegious anti-Jewish or anti-Christian acts of the ISIS Muslims. But there is something horribly grim in the media spectacle of these tribal rites, in this baroque cult of desecration.

There is something horribly grim, in particular, in the ways in which the Israeli genocide takes place: although the Israelis' actions revisit the trauma of the Holocaust, the gothic severity of the German murderers appears lost in them.

The postmodern return of genocide lacks the impassive rigor with which the blonde beast pursued his inhumane plan.

Mediatized and popularized, today's extermination arouses the psychotic joy of the murderers of the Israel Defense Forces, and excites the cheerful arrogance of the civilian army of settlers.

Rigorously nationalized in the gothic Hitler era, holocaust now becomes, in the neoliberal era, a private enterprise, and a comedic entertainment for the Israeli families who delight in looking at the images of the torturers who happily carry out their vile work.

After having witnessed the bombing of a civilian population, we witnessed the spectacle of a cheerful people in arms, thirsty for blood, massacring a population of desperate people, chasing families fleeing from one tent city to another.

Mediatized horror has become a daily spectacle, savagery is part of the carnival, and the vulgar baroque of the brainless masses has taken the place of the haughty gothic of the past century, while waiting for someone to turn off the megascreen.

This type of violence has no other purpose than to humiliate, dehumanize, and above all inflict pain. Therefore it goes beyond ferocity, the natural reflex of an attacked, terrified animal body, which is motivated only by the instinct of survival.

In this type of violence there is something exquisitely human, psychologically elaborate: cruelty, the pleasure of subjugating and inflicting pain.

This pleasure of doing evil is not ferocity, but it is a particular manifestation of ferocity, in which the perverse desire becomes predominant over the need to protect oneself.

Zionism is not only the policy of ferocious self-defense of a collective body that has not freed itself from the trauma of the Holocaust but it is also the perverse policy of a colonialist state, of a population of settlers who take advantage of the suffering suffered in the past by their ancestors, who exploit their own privilege, and who enjoy the pain inflicted on those who cannot defend themselves.

Hier Ist Kein Warum

The heirs of Holocaust victims seize land from the Palestinians and violently expropriate them.

They chase entire families out of their homes, they break down doors with their boots, they hit farmers who are defending their belongings with the butts of their rifles.

Is this compensation for everything that the Jews suffered a hundred years ago, five hundred years ago, a thousand years ago?

We can understand this.

The greater the brutality suffered in the past, the greater the brutality of present behavior.

But then we must also understand the violence of the Hamas militants who on October 7, finally, were able to behave with the families of Sderot, with the young Israelis who listened to music, as the Israelis have behaved with them for seventy-five years.

If I understand the violence of the Israelis, I must also understand that of the Palestinians.

Understand.

What does understanding mean in these cases?

It means understanding the causes, the origins, the reasons that are not reasons.

There is no reason in history—this is the lesson we learn from the Gaza holocaust.

"*Hier ist kein warum*," writes Primo Levi in his novel *If This Is a Man*.[2]

In Auschwitz, a Nazi soldier prevents a thirsty inmate from putting a piece of frozen snow to his lips. The inmate asks him why.

The answer is this: "There is no why here," there is no reason here.[3]

Understanding does not mean sharing the reasons, because there are no reasons, just a psychotic chain. Understanding means going back up the chain of psychotic automatisms.

There is no reason in history; reason has nothing to do with history, regardless of what was said by German philosophers who thought that History was the place for the implementation of Reason.

But now philosophy is silent, it has nothing more to say.

It is not reason that explains the events of history, particularly its tragedies; only trauma processing can explain anything.

Idealistic interpretations explain the historical process on the basis of values, programs, ideals: purposes that exist and often occupy the visible scene, but are actually nothing but epiphenomena.

History draws its destructive energy from the process of processing trauma.

Political action, much more than the pursuit of ideals and programs, is the construction of institutions that aim to process a past trauma and avoid its recurrence.

All the political rhetoric that followed 1945 can be ultimately seen as an attempt to prevent the horror from returning by the construction of international institutions of mediation and of peacekeeping.

This attempt has definitively failed after October 7, because the problem of how to process past trauma has never really been addressed.

Politics does not have tools for this processing, which alone can prevent the conditions of violence from recurring and the trauma from reproducing.

Pain is at the core of this chain, but political reason absolutely ignores what to do with pain: political reason ignores how to talk about it or understand it, let alone cure it.

Political reason is very much about justice, about law, but is unable to deal with pain.

Only Christianity has put pain at the center of its meditation, only Christianity has staged a god who becomes human and experiences pain.

The God of the Old Testament doesn't care about pain; on the contrary, when he can, the God of the Old Testament enjoys humans' pain.

Pain makes no sense in the Old Testament, as Job learns the hard way. The only meaning of pain is the pleasure and satisfaction of the psychotic God of the Old Testament.

There is no reason in this story. Reason is only a superficial explanation of structural interests and deep emotions.

Interests sometimes manage to shine through in the discourse of politics, which constructs its plots to defend the interests of the dominant against the interests of the dominated.

But emotions remain irrelevant for historical reason, so they are handed over to religion, or to psychoanalysis, which does not dare to stick its nose into political matters.

This is why the trauma of history ends up fueling an infinite chain of revenge. As W. H. Auden writes in "September 1, 1939":

> I and the public know
> What all schoolchildren learn,
> Those to whom evil is done
> Do evil in return.[4]

The comparison between Israel and German Nazism is dizzying to the point of appearing repugnant. It is a taboo that one does not dare violate, because violating it means exposing oneself to a reaction of moral censorship.

If we do not violate this taboo, however, we will miss something essential for the historical and above all psychological understanding of what has happened and what will happen in the history of Israel in its relationship with the Palestinians.

The identification with the executioner is a well-known psychological process: every mistreated or abused child, when grown up, tends to reproduce the behaviors that hurt them, because they were indelibly inscribed in their developing mind.

In the same way, those who have suffered traumatic violence can be led (only in some cases, let it be clear) to identify with the perpetrator of the violence: they can desire that strength, that dominance.

But even if we avoid resorting to psychoanalysis, there is a much more concrete reason why it is good to identify with the executioner, to the point of actually becoming the executioner: the only way to save yourself from Nazism is to be a Nazi.

The Israelis, heirs of those who suffered the trauma of the Holocaust, realized that the only way to protect themselves from Nazism was to adopt the techniques of Nazism, and to acquire the ruthlessness of the Nazi.

Those who established the State of Israel were aware they had to face enemies who had learned something from Nazism: for reasons linked to the fight against British colonialism, Arab nationalism had a declared affinity to Nazi fascism.

For this reason, the decision to establish a state in the territory of Palestine exposed the Israelis to a dilemma from the beginning: suffer the armed violence of those who (predictably) did not want a Zionist state to be established on the territory of the Palestinian Arabs, or be strong enough to crush Arab nationalism and to reduce the Palestinian population to subjugation, forever removing any possibility of self-determination.

Zionism could only choose the path of force.

Thanks to the support of Western countries, the Zionists become a military power, and the military superiority of the State of Israel in turn pushed the Palestinians to practice terrorism.

Only an internationalist and poststatist option could therefore have avoided war, but Zionism is based on the rejection of the internationalist culture that had been predominant in Jewish politics until the 1930s, but had not avoided the Nazi extermination.

The defeat of internationalism and the defeat of diasporic cosmopolitanism are at the origin of the interminable clash between the nascent State of Israel and the Arab states—just as they are at the origin of every other tragedy that has devastated the world in the twentieth century, and even more in the first quarter of the twenty-first century.

Psychic Contagion

"Since the war began"—since the genocide began—"mental health professional and author Merav Roth ... has been treating people for trauma. Now she fears the disaster's consequences for society: 'The desire to take revenge on everybody is very dangerous for us.'"[5]

The documentary *Born in Gaza*, directed by Hernán Zin and available on Netflix, tells the story of ten children between the ages of six and fourteen during the 2014 war—one of the many wars that Israel has waged against the Palestinians, and that the Palestinians have conducted against Israel. These children talk about the bombings, the wounds they received, the terror they experience every day, the hunger they suffer. They say that their existence is not life, that dying would be better.

It is likely that these people who were children in 2014 are now Hamas militants, and that they participated in the orgy of terror on October 7. How can you not understand it? If I were in their place, instead of mine—that of an old white intellectual who is writing comfortably, sitting in his house in an Italian city where for the moment there are no bombings—if I were one of these children bombed in 2014, today I would be a terrorist who only aspired to kill an Israeli. Would I be horrified by myself?

Of course I would be horrified. But my calm pacifism is just a privilege I enjoy because I didn't live my childhood in Gaza, or in many other places like Gaza.

Therefore Israel has only one way to eradicate Hamas: kill all the Palestinians living in Gaza, in the occupied territories, and elsewhere; everyone, everyone, everyone, especially the children. After all, that's what they're doing, right? It's called genocide, but it's completely rational.

In fact, the very rational rulers of Europe support the genocide.

The German Chancellor, Olaf Scholz, has said that since Germany committed genocide in the past, it is now its duty to support those who are committing genocide today. It seems like it's the only way to make amends.

It's the only way to eradicate terrorism, right?

Perhaps there could be another way to eradicate it: unconditional peace; a renunciation of winning;

friendship, desertion, alliance between the victims, the victims of Hitler and the victims of Netanyahu. But this is the resolution of someone who is too naive, a resolution based on feelings that can only be nourished when one finds oneself in a condition of privilege. In real life, it seems that the victims only aspire to become executioners. And they often succeed. Therefore the spiral will not stop, and we do not know which vortex it is destined to fuel.

There is something monstrous in the minds of the Palestinians who have lived in terror. And there is something equally monstrous in the minds of the Israelis.

But how can we judge the behavior of peoples? How can we judge the explosions of violence that multiply in collective life?

Can we judge the behavior of Hamas militants or that of Israelis in ethical terms, or in political terms?

Ethical reason is off the table, because ethics has been totally erased from the collective panorama of our time and from the conscience of the great majority.

Ethics is the evaluation of action from the point of view of the good of the other as a continuation of the self. But in the conditions of generalized war in which humanity that has survived the human moves, the other is only the enemy. It is the effect of the liberal-competitive infection, and of the nationalist infection: the defense of physical and imaginary territory becomes war.

Ethics is dead, and piety is dead. There is no ethics in the behavior of young people who grew up in the prison of Gaza, because their minds cannot consider the other (the Israeli soldier who awaits them, with his weapon drawn, at every crossroads) except as a jailer, torturer, mortal enemy. Each social fragment (people, ethnicity, mafia, organization, party, family, individual) is desperately fighting for its own survival, like a wolf fighting against other wolves. The video game instructs us to compete in conditions of hyperaccelerated, ubiquitous warfare.

Like ethical reason, political reason is no longer relevant in a situation in which strategic decision-making is replaced by microdecisions of immediate survival.

Israel reacts to Hamas's brutal violence in a way that may or may not be militarily effective, but is certainly not politically effective.

The Israeli rulers are corrupt mafiosi famous for their long-lasting cynicism and opportunism. After October 7, they found themselves faced with a situation that they had not even imagined, even if they had carefully prepared for it. But if Israeli fascists such as Netanyahu, Ben-Gvir, and Smotrich were able to quickly turn the massacre of their fellow citizens into an opportunity to strengthen their power and expand their territory, the entire people of Israel have lost their minds. They have kept their technical capacity for extermination intact, but they have lost the sense of belonging to the human race, the sense of *pietas*—or rather, the feeling of empathy without which every crime is legitimized because its horror is not perceived.

Everything in the behavior of the Israelis proves that a psychotic crisis is underway, which has and will continue to hurt the Palestinians a lot, but which will also hurt the Israelis a lot.

Genocidal Intention

> Many of my friends recognise the injustice of the occupation, and … profess a "love for humanity." But at this moment, under these circumstances, this is not what they are focused on. Instead, they feel that in the struggle between justice and existence, existence must win out, and in the struggle between one just cause and another—that of the Israelis and that of the Palestinians—it is our own cause that must be triumphant, no matter the price. To those who doubt this stark choice, the Holocaust is presented as the alternative, however irrelevant it is to the current moment.
>
> This feeling did not appear suddenly on October 7. Its roots are much deeper.[6]

In no way can we deny or forget the violence committed by Hamas on that day.

I know that international law considers armed resistance against an occupying power to be legitimate (and Israel is a power that occupies the territory where millions of Palestinians live). But I am not interested in this consideration, because October 7 was—technically speaking—a pogrom against a population that has a long memory of the pogrom.

I therefore do not intend to defend in any way the

right of Hamas to carry out the atrocities committed on October 7.

But I defend the right to ask who is responsible for the extreme of exasperation and humiliation to which the Palestinians have been led after seventy-five years of oppression.

It is not a question of legality. International law legitimizes the armed resistance of a people undergoing occupation, but I don't deal with law. I deal with pain, humiliation, and desperation: that's what I'm about.

If we didn't know anything about the history of the Nakba and the seventy-five years that followed the violent occupation of the land on which one and a half million Palestinians lived, if we didn't know anything about the prolonged imprisonment of two million citizens of Gaza, if we didn't know anything about the illegal settlements of those who have expelled the Palestinians living in the West Bank with threats of violence and murder, if we didn't know anything about the concentration camps for refugees in which the occupiers locked up hundreds of thousands of Palestinians—in short, if we knew nothing about what happened before October 7—then what happened after October 7 would be enough to open our eyes to reality, would force us to recognize that Israel is a hyperarmed power that pursues a colonial and racist policy, which from the beginning has been able to exist only thanks to the military and political support of British and American imperialism, thanks to systematic violence against the population living in the area.

Palestinians have been forced to abandon their homes, their forms of life; they have been obliged to forget their history of secularism and tolerance. They have been put in a position of rebelling in conditions of absolute military disadvantage, and in some cases forced (yes, I repeat, forced) to resort to terrorism as the only way to exist.

The attack of October 7 was atrocious but inevitable and politically effective—it is terrible to say it, but it must be said—because only after that action was world public opinion faced with the truth that Israel had been hiding for decades, the truth that the entire West wanted to ignore.

What happened after October 7 served to retrospectively illuminate what the West did not want to see: after months of inconceivable cruelty and revolting cynicism, anyone who is not being entirely in bad faith was forced to recognize that Israel contradicts all the principles on which liberal democracy and international legality are founded (were founded).

After what happened, anyone who is not being in bad faith must recognize that peace can only return to the area when the State of Israel has been erased from the map. The tale of "two peoples, two states" only served to cover the policy of occupation and extermination. No one ever believed it because it was never credible. And in any case, the creation of two states would simply mean the acceptance of the nationalist and fascist principle according to which the state corresponds to the ethnic or religious identity of a population.

After October 7, the ferocity of the IDF fully unfolded, and the Israeli civilians put on a show of unimaginable cruelty: aiming to starve the Palestinian population, they blocked the trucks at the Gaza crossings.

Settlers armed by Minister Bezalel Smotrich carried out daily attacks against Palestinian families in the West Bank; destroyed Palestinian homes, land, and olive trees; and forcibly expelled inhabitants, imprisoned young men, and killed those who tried to resist.

Furthermore, Israeli and European rulers have accused of anti-Semitism anyone who denounces the genocidal intention of the IDF and of the Israeli government and population. The genocidal intention is evident in the systematic massacre of those who cannot be accused of complicity with Hamas, such as the children who were slaughtered by the thousands in bombings and also in targeted actions.

The genocidal intention is manifest in the blockade of humanitarian aid that has brought the population of Gaza to the brink of famine. It is manifest in the destruction of wells that has deprived Gazans of water for drinking and washing.

The genocidal intention is undeniable if you consider the fact that doctors and health care personnel have been hit, arrested, and killed.

The genocidal intention was clear and openly declared from the first day of indiscriminate aggression, as anyone knows well after reading the statements of the political and military leaders of the State of Israel.

2

IN DARKNESS

"These people there deserve death, a hard death, an agonizing death, and instead we see them enjoying on the beach and having fun," complained Mr. Shlezinger, the religious affairs correspondent for the widely circulated right-wing *Israel Hayom* newspaper. "We should have seen a lot more revenge there," Mr. Shlezinger unrepentantly added. "A lot more rivers of Gazans' blood."

It would be nice to think that Mr. Shlezinger is a fringe figure or that Israelis would be shocked by his bloody fantasies. But he's not, and many wouldn't be.

Israel has hardened, and the signs of it are in plain view. Dehumanizing language and promises of annihilation from military and political leaders. Polls that found wide support for the policies that have wreaked devastation and starvation in Gaza. Selfies of Israeli soldiers preening proudly in bomb-crushed Palestinian neighborhoods.[1]

Megan K. Stack, in *The New York Times*, reports that some rappers widely listened to by young Israelis are calling for annihilation, and preaching that there will be no mercy for the "rats": "They will die in their rat holes."[2]

Many stores display products with the words "Finish them" written on them.[3] Literal translation: *exterminate them*.

How is it possible that Israel has become the lair of a people of ferocious and death-hungry murderers? Israel has not always been like this, even if the state entity conceived by the Zionists and protected by the British and the Americans was born as a foreign and hostile body that, since 1948, has generated uninterrupted violence.

Regardless of what well-intentioned Zionists say, the State of Israel was from the beginning an artificial construction that could only be sustained by oppression and by violence.

But only in recent years has that abusive and violent state been fully transformed into an extermination machine, which after October 7 revealed its repugnant face that now everyone in the world is obliged to see with horror.

It is clear that we are dealing with a psychotic collapse shared by an entire population, a collapse that in my opinion heralds the disintegration of the Zionist entity.

The coming collapse will be provoked by the understanding that the dream of living a peaceful life alongside the hell of millions of people is an evil dream, impossible to realize.

It is now crystal clear that that place in which the Europeans managed to trap the Jews after having exterminated them in the 1940s, far from being a safe place, is the most dangerous place in the world for the Jews. It is a trap: the continuation of the death machine that Nazism built for the Jews of Europe.

In the same sense, Zionism is the continuation of the Final Solution conceived by the Nazis.

After October 7, white supremacists and Zionists find themselves facing a world that is thirsty for revenge, and is becoming ungovernable.

White supremacy's days are numbered, because the oppressed world has the technical ability to build the same instruments of death that the West has. The Global South is acquiring all the technical tools that are necessary to carry out attacks on the besieged colonialist citadel.

I am obviously referring to weapons, including nuclear weapons, that are no longer the prerogative of the great white powers—the United States and Russia—but are also the property of countries in the southern hemisphere, starting with North Korea, Pakistan, India, and of course China.

Nuclear proliferation is a serious danger for the future of humankind (second, perhaps, only to climate change). The fact that technical knowledge is no longer seized by predators makes their superiority increasingly fragile, and the Palestinian issue is the litmus test of this reversal of power relations at a planetary level.

Let's look at the map: let's see which countries recognize the Palestinian state and which countries do not recognize it, and we will have proof of the fact that the white Zionists are a besieged minority.

The besieged are hyperarmed, but this is the only advantage they have. This superiority will not last forever.

Who Is Amalek?

In one of his speeches, Netanyahu cited Amalek, a biblical character who recurs in songs of Nazi-Zionist rappers but also in neo-Biblical delusions circulating in Israeli public discourse.

But who is this Amalek?

When the Jews freed themselves from the slavery they had suffered for generations in Egypt, they headed toward the Promised Land but were attacked by the Amalekites, a tribe that had settled in their absence in the Negev desert.

Amalek was the nephew of Esau, and was the patriarch who led that tribe.

This story is told in the Bible, that scary book that has always contributed to shaping the Western mind according to the style of a homicidal obsession.

The mythologem of Amalek has always remained in the background of Jewish history, an imaginary projection that is embodied in the persecutors of the Jewish people, from Emperor Titus to the Cossack General Khmelnytsky, up to Hitler and up to Sinwar, the head of Hamas.

Uttering the name of Amalek is dangerous, and should not be done lightly. Riccardo Paredi, a scholar at the American University of Beirut, writes:

> In the passage cited by Netanyahu, the Hebrew Bible twice orders the Israelites to "erase" the memory (*zekher*) of Amalek. ... The biblical trope of "remembering"—especially of passing a divine teaching from generation to generation—is well known (the imperative *zachor* appears 169 times in the Hebrew Bible). ... And it is a paradoxical reminder. With such a command, "inconsistency is inevitable": do not forget to erase the memory of your enemy. Remember to forget. But how can you forget something you were ordered to remember?[4]

The State of Israel was founded from the beginning on a vengeful obsession with memory. Naturally the same could be said of any nation-state, because nations are always born from an obsessive deformation of memory, but in the case of Israel, the biblical obsession of the *zekher* has been welded to the psychotic way of processing the trauma of the Holocaust.

In 2018, the secular State of Israel was transformed into the "state of the Jews": nationalism and fundamentalism became the governing force, completing the slow sociocultural transformation of the Israeli population. Since the 1990s, many intellectuals, students, and people with a secular or socialist orientation had left the country, to be replaced by a mass who came from the countries of the disintegrating Eastern Bloc, and who had the aim of occupying land without the problems of conscience tormenting the Jews of European descent.

Furthermore, the most fanatical Israeli citizens give birth to many children, while those who were not obsessed with identity give birth to few. This is why Israel has turned into the aggressive monster that the whole world has seen in action in recent months.

After the assassination of Yitzhak Rabin by an extremist settler in 1995, after the provocation of Ariel Sharon, who in the year 2000 claimed Israeli sovereignty over the Temple Mount with a not at all peaceful walk, Israel has changed for the worse, and this change seems to be irreversible.

Netanyahu is the product of this mutation, and at the same time he is the clearest expression of the cynicism that arises from the fusion of racist colonialism with religious fundamentalism. Against this background, we must understand the language with which Netanyahu threw fuel on the fire of October 7, aware of the fact that by exacerbating the war he could postpone the moment of reckoning before the judges and the world.

In his essay, Riccardo Paredi writes: "By interpreting the divine command in a literal and fundamentalist way, as Netanyahu does, the 'erasure of the memory' of Amalek from under the sky, under penalty of one's own defeat, is a divine obligation. In modern terms, God commands genocide."[5]

Since the State of Israel has been based on a hypertrophy of memory, Israel tends to identify the figure of Amalek with those who have inhabited this land for centuries. The very existence of Israel, in the long run, demands the extermination of the Palestinian children of Amalek.

Anyone who disapproves of the actions of the State of Israel is Amalek—that is, an enemy of the Jews.

The Palestinians are the last, most recent incarnation of the Amalekites, because they took advantage of the (two thousand year) absence of the Jews to occupy part of their land.

In the name of memory—or rather, in the name of mythology—Zionism claimed to dislodge these Amalekites, not recognizing their existence.

This mythological delirium has been turned into historical truth. As a consequence, the Palestinians have been persecuted, hidden from view beyond a wall, confined to detention camps, and finally eliminated by fire.

But on October 7, the repressed returned to the scene, and now, whatever happens, they cannot be erased again.

Unless Israel completes the genocide to perfection, physically eliminating several million people, the Zionist entity cannot win, given the premises with which Netanyahu started the war in Gaza, which is not a war but a genocide (for the moment, imperfect).

This is why I believe that the end of Israel is underway.

The Wolf Is Not Dead

To defend the colonialist Zionist entity, the Israelis have committed another affront, which will perhaps be the most fatal for them. They have allied themselves with the worst anti-Semites ever—Christian racists of the US Republican right, European fascists, and so on. Together, they have trivialized the accusation of anti-Semitism, using this very serious charge as a weapon, as blackmail, as a barroom insult.

They have gone as far as accusing of anti-Semitism the judge of the International Court of Justice, they have gone as far as accusing of anti-Semitism Jewish intellectuals who protested against the genocide.

This is bad and this is dangerous, because it's not safe to cry wolf when the wolf isn't there. The students waving the Palestinian flag at American universities are not the wolf (in fact, many of them are Jewish).

The problem is that the wolf has not disappeared, and he may appear again.

The wolf has put on his good suit and tie. He is hiding among the Trumpist Republicans who shout "Long live Israel," he is hiding among the Italian fascists who send the police to beat pro-Palestine students, he is hiding among the French descendants of Pétain.

But as the saying goes, *il lupo perde il pelo ma non il vizio* (the wolf loses its fur but not its vice), and anti-Semitism is destined to reemerge sooner or later.

It is easy to foresee that the inhumanity of Israel's behavior will generate a wave of hatred that for now unfolds in the forms of peaceful protest, but tomorrow could turn into a new persecution of the Jews.

Israel is the creation of a group of Zionists with little foresight, but above all it is the creation of Europeans, who took the opportunity offered by the Zionists to get rid of the Jews. After killing six million Jews, the Europeans then pretended to have become friends with them and spewed them out from Europe.

"Spew" is not my word, but that of Amos Oz, who in his memoir *A Tale of Love and Darkness* writes:

> Some of our friends and neighbors encouraged themselves ... with the comforting thought that even if the Arabs didn't want us here, the last thing the peoples of Europe wanted was for us to go back and flood Europe again. And since the Europeans were far more powerful than the Arabs, it followed that there was a chance that we might be left here after all. They would force the Arabs to swallow what Europe was trying to spew forth.[6]

The Jews spewed out by the Europeans, and relocated in a desert fraught with danger, were eventually used by the Anglo-Americans as a Western outpost in the region that for decades has been the West's main supplier of much-needed oil.

But in a not so distant future, the hatred that Israel has fostered in the Middle East may fuel a wave of real anti-Semitism, and then the game could change: the European fascists and the American Trumpists could get tired of having to defend those Jews who, in reality, they have never stopped despising.

And then it will be futile to cry wolf.

Gaza Is Auschwitz with Cameras

Auschwitz was the scientific exercise of all techniques aimed at extermination. It was prolonged and uninterrupted torture, the systematic use of terror against a population of inmates who had no chance of escaping. It was the unleashing of tremendous firepower against a defenseless, disarmed, naked population. It was the intentional pursuit of genocide, the systematic murder of innocents, of women, of children.

What the Israelis are doing in Gaza, what the Israelis have been doing for decades throughout the territory of Palestine, has the same quality of cruelty and scientific precision. Everything that has been said and written about Auschwitz can be said and written again about Gaza.

The siege causes hunger, thirst, the deprivation of everything essential for survival. The bombings inflict constant terror on innocent people who run from one side to the other without knowing where to take refuge.

Ethnic discrimination, deportation, torture, extermination: this defines Hitler's Nazism, and we regularly find this in the behavior of the Israeli army.

The entire Israeli population (with very few exceptions) participated in the extermination of the

Palestinians, just as the entire German population (with very few exceptions) participated in the extermination of the Jews.

These are not two equatable events, however, because there is a huge difference between that and this.

The difference between Auschwitz and Gaza lies in the public, proudly ostentatious nature of the suffering inflicted on the Palestinians. The lesson that the Zionists are teaching the world is that there is no way to defend our lives, our parents, and our children, there is no way to escape the unchained violence of a state that makes systematic use of ethnic cleansing techniques, apartheid, and mass deportation.

Gaza is not like Auschwitz, because in those camps back then there were no cameras, while today the whole of humanity sits in the living room and observes on-screen its own future, foretold in the present reality of Gaza and Jenin.

It's hard to say what effect this display of horror is going produce on the minds of the new generation, of the children who witness every day the torture and mutilations that Israel inflicts on their Palestinian peers.

Once upon a time, when we talked about counter-information, when we organized radio stations and websites to denounce evil, we believed that showing violence and denouncing murderers could help isolate and shame them, and ultimately could reduce injustice.

Ultimately I've been led to realize that the visibility of evil is not necessarily helpful to getting free from it.

Once upon a time, I was persuaded that free information and media activism could be a check on the aggressiveness of an authoritarian state. Back then, I thought that a thousand street journalists witnessing in words and in images the brutality of the police, the violence against migrants might be a check on the criminality of power.

What is happening now is much more complex, and in some regards it is the opposite of what I had believed and hoped.

Violence has become visible, but this visibility works in a dual way: on the one hand, it arouses horrified emotions; on the other, it spreads fear and a feeling of impotence to the point of inducing identification with the aggressor.

The orgy of horror on small and large screens that is haunting us in every place and at every hour of the day produces, among other things, a sort of visual nihilism: an aesthetic addiction to horror.

It is becoming increasingly difficult to distinguish between fiction and reality. The reality of genocide has the same visual quality as the horror movies and video games to which this generation has been exposed from early childhood. What kind of internal worldview is forming in the minds of this unfortunate generation?

Reenacting their own extermination seems to be the irresistible drive of the Israeli people: better to be on the side of the exterminator than on the side of the exterminated.

The black wave that is spreading across the world has thrived on the proliferation of images, because hypermediatization has accelerated the pace of information stimulus, spreading panic and making society incapable of reacting. In panic, the collective organism clings to the reassurance of identity, but this is completely artificial, because in metropolitan life there is no more community, and identity is an effect of fictitious reaction.

The only truly existing thing, the only sentiment in the heart of those who have grown up viewing horror stories since early childhood, is the despair of a collective organism searching for reassurance in a collective ritual of hatred.

Collapse, Panic

At the end of the pandemic, when the bio-virus receded, the psycho-virus exploded: war spread to every corner of planetary existence.

In *A Thousand Plateaus*, Deleuze and Guattari succinctly define fascism as a situation in which war is in every niche.[7] Therefore we can say that humanity has entered a sort of techno-fascism, a biopolitical process of extermination.

The Ukrainian war and the Israeli genocide demonstrate that no rational defense, no international institution can stop the proliferation of the fascist virus, injected by war into the social organism.

Moshe Dayan once said that Israel must act "like a mad dog," so that its enemies will know that their hostile actions will receive an immense response: a strategy that infinitely expands upon the biblical code of "an eye for an eye."[8]

Hit schools, hospitals, everything: kill, kill, kill.

I wonder if Israel's leaders realize the effects that this tsunami of horror will have on the global psycho-sphere.

Months and months of continuous horror have erased the horror of October 7 from the collective psyche, and have produced conditions for a monstrous mutation in the perception of Israel by the planetary mind.

From a clinical perspective, the vast majority of Israelis today appear as psychopaths who have lost all moral inhibition, and are therefore dangerous for others but also for themselves, and for those who have handed their destiny over to them.

The entire West, for reasons that have nothing noble about them (the sense of guilt linked to the Holocaust, which has transformed into a negative identity for Europe), has handed its destiny over to Israel.

There have been other massacres in the past, and in the present—but none of them has so completely occupied the media-sphere and consequently the psycho-sphere of the entire planet.

What consequences do the Israeli avengers expect from this spectacle, beyond the unlikely annihilation of Hamas?

Is it possible to display the tortured body of an entire population on screens across the planet without arousing hatred in all those who are not part of the supremacist minority?

Nobody knows how the political-military situation is destined to evolve.

We can assume that the Arab states, much more attentive to the wallets of the nationalist elites than to Islamic solidarity, will continue with their hypocritical condemnations without giving up trade and agreements with Israel. This is not the price Israel will pay. The Western establishment and the Arab establishment will not break with the Zionist entity.

But Israel will pay the price of moral disintegration, and of mental mayhem.

Israel's ruling class is steeped in cynicism and arrogance; in order to maintain control of the situation, it will not back down in the face of any crime, but it will not be able to maintain that control for long, because the martyrdom of the Palestinians is the moral catastrophe of the Israelis.

The Jewish consciousness will not be able to coexist for long with the responsibility for a genocide.

In the first days of the genocide, the American Jewish community occupied the halls of Capitol Hill and the pedestal of the Statue of Liberty to declare "Not in our name," to refuse their identification with those in Israel who are carrying out the extermination.[9]

Then countless Jewish intellectuals denounced the cynical use of October 7 as a tool for pursuing a project of annexation and of deportation.

In an article titled "Israel Takes Its Last Breath," the well-known writer Ari Shavit writes:

> It appears we have passed the point of no return, and it may be that "Israel" can no longer end the

> occupation, stop colonization, or achieve peace. It seems impossible to reform Zionism, save democracy, and divide the people of this land. …
>
> If the situation is as it is, then:
>
> • There is no reason to live in this country.
>
> • There is no reason to write in *Haaretz.*
>
> • There is no reason to read *Haaretz.*
>
> We must follow what Rogel Alpher suggested two years ago—leave the country … If "Israelism" and Jewishness are no longer a vital part of one's identity, and if every Israeli citizen holds a foreign passport, not only technically but psychologically, then it's over. We should say goodbye to our friends and move to San Francisco, Berlin, or Paris.
>
> From there, from the land of new German nationa-lism or new American nationalism, we should calmly watch as the "State of Israel" takes its last breath.
>
> We must take three steps back and watch the Jewish democratic state sink.[10]

Israel is no longer (if it ever was) a representation of Judaism; it is its shame, its reversed image.

The Israeli genocide is arousing fear and hatred in those populations that have memories of colonial humiliation, while Europeans look the other way as the massacre takes place so close by.

Europeans did the same in the 1930s and 1940s, when genocide was taking place on their soil, but not, as is the case today, under their mediatized eyes.

Despite the cynical support that the leaders of Europe and the United States have guaranteed to the Israeli genocide, the youth of Europe and North America have identified with the Palestinians, and have marched in solidarity not so much for historical and political reasons but for the perception of a common claustrophobic condition, the intuition of a common absence of a future.

It is this despair, this absence of a future and of hope, that makes the Palestinians the vanguard of the new generation worldwide.

The Betrayal of Jewish Culture

It is impossible to describe Israel's horrible mutation without referring to the original trauma, the Holocaust. The desire for revenge has little to do with politics, a lot to do with psychopathology.

The mad dog is truly mad; we need to understand the genesis of his madness, which emerged not after October 7 but long before. This point is extremely delicate and painful: the evolution of the Israeli unconscious, in increasing contradiction to Jewish history and culture.

Before his death in 1967, Isaac Deutscher wrote about Judaism caught in the trap of the nation-state: "The world has compelled the Jew to embrace the nation-state and to make of it his pride and hope just at a time when there is little or no hope left in it. You cannot blame the Jews for this; you must blame the world. But Jews should at least be aware of the paradox and realize that their intense enthusiasm for 'national sovereignty' is historically belated."[11]

Deutscher's warning was not heeded: the part of the Jewish community that identified with Israel ended up believing that only a strong, exclusive, hyperarmed nation-state could defend them. This is a serious mistake, but it is not certain that the Israeli people will break free of this mistake before ending up at the bottom of the abyss.

Since 1948, the existence of Israel has coincided with the betrayal of modern Jewish culture. Israel wants to be a nation, and for this reason it sets in motion the expulsion, deportation, internment, and subjugation of the population present on that territory.

Israel has won one war after another, destroyed Palestinian organizations, enhanced its military power, and built an atomic arsenal so as to became unbeatable militarily.

Nevertheless, the nation-state of Israel is the trap in which the Europeans have locked the Jews. From the point of view of people's well-being, life in Israel is a claustrophobic hell. And from the point of view of the geopolitical long run, the gift from the English colonialists, promised by Balfour in 1917 and delivered in 1948, is now revealing itself for what it has been from the beginning: a poisoned gift.

The Palestinians have entered the dead-end tunnel of the nation-state.

The formula "two peoples, two states" sanctioned the identitarian and tribal character of the nation-state and denied any possibility of peaceful coexistence between two communities within a single political entity.

Both state entities (the existing one of Israel and the nonexistent but proclaimed one of Palestine) have ended up identifying with their more identitarian, fundamentalist, religious, or openly fascist components.

This is why the nation-state of Israel is a betrayal of the Jewish legacy of cosmopolitan nomadism. But the State of Israel also represents the betrayal of Jewish culture from another point of view, which Giorgio Agamben captures with extreme acuteness in a September 2024 article titled "The End of Judaism":

> One cannot understand the meaning of what is taking place in Israel today if one does not understand that Zionism constitutes a double negation of the historical reality of Judaism. Not only does it in fact transfer to the Jews the nation-state of Christians, but Zionism represents the culmination of that process of assimilation which, since the late 18th century, has been gradually canceling Jewish identity. Decisively, as Amnon Raz-Krakotzkin has shown in an exemplary study, at the foundation of Zionist consciousness lies another negation, the negation of Galut, that is, of exile as a principle common to all historical forms of Judaism as we know it. The premises of this conception of exile predate the destruction of the Second Temple and are already present in biblical literature. Exile is the very form of Jewish existence on Earth, and the

entire Jewish tradition—from the Mishnah to the Talmud, from the architecture of the synagogue to the memory of biblical events—was conceived and lived from the perspective of exile. For an Orthodox Jew, Jews living in the state of Israel are also in exile. And the state according to the Torah, which Jews await upon the coming of the Messiah, has nothing to do with a modern nation-state, so much so that at its core lie precisely the rebuilding of the Temple and the restoration of sacrifices, which the state of Israel does not even want to hear about.

And we should not forget that exile according to Judaism is not only the condition of the Jews, but concerns the deficient condition of the world as a whole. According to some Kabbalists, including Luria, exile defines the very situation of divinity, which created the world by exiling itself from itself, and this exile will last until the advent of Tiqqun, that is, the restoration of the original order.

It is precisely this unconditional acceptance of exile, with the rejection it entails of all present forms of statehood, that establishes the superiority of Jews over religions and peoples who have compromised with the state. Jews are, along with the Roma, the only people who have rejected the state form, conducted no wars, and never stained themselves with the blood of other peoples.

In its fundamental denial of exile and diaspora in favor of a nation-state, Zionism has therefore betrayed the very essence of Judaism. Small wonder then that this removal produced another exile, that of the Palestinians, and led the state of Israel to identify itself with the most extreme and ruthless forms of the modern nation-state. The tenacious claim of history, from which the Diaspora according to Zionists would have excluded Jews, points in the same direction. But this may mean that Judaism, which had not died at Auschwitz, perhaps meets its end today.[12]

Genocide

Remember Srebrenica? The Serbian nationalists led by Ratko Mladić and Radovan Karadžić, after separating adult men from women and children, massacred eight thousand Bosniaks under the eyes of the United Nations. The International Court of Justice convicted Mladić and Karadžić of genocide.

Thirty years later, under the eyes of the United Nations, the Israel Defense Forces massacred fifty thousand Palestinians in Gaza without even doing the courtesy of distinguishing (as the war criminal Mladić did) between men, women, and children.

According to the definition adopted by the United Nations, the word *genocide* refers to "acts committed with intent to destroy, in whole or in part, a national, ethnical, racial or religious group."[13]

The word *genocide* was first introduced by Raphael Lemkin, a Polish jurist of Jewish origin, and used in the indictments of the Nuremberg Tribunal that charged the Nazis with conducting a "deliberate and systematic genocide, viz. the extermination of racial and national groups, against the civilian population of certain occupied territories to destroy particular races and classes of people, and national, racial or religious groups, particularly, Jews, Poles and Gypsies and others."[14]

Given these premises, it is difficult—indeed, impossible—to deny that Israel is carrying out a genocide against the Palestinian population.

Anyone who denies it is in bad faith.

It can be considered that the extermination following October 7 was justified as a reaction, albeit disproportionate, to that massacre.

After the events that have followed October 7, after the genocide conducted by Israel, the problem of the ethical and legal legitimacy of Israel's existence as a state arises again, and this time it can no longer be evaded. What we have tried to hide in these seventy-five years is that the State of Israel openly constitutes itself as a genocidal entity.

The formulation "a land without a people for a people without a land" was more than a falsehood. It was not only a lie, since in that land a people existed and continues to exist and resist, but it also revealed a declared intention of genocide.

Whoever is in the land that God has promised to us will be deported or eliminated so that the chosen people can return to where they lived two millennia ago.

Chaim Weizmann's declaration that the right of the Jews to territorialize Palestine (and therefore to deport or eliminate those living there) is based on "memory" implies genocide as a logical corollary of the biblical premise.[15]

3

LET'S DO AWAY WITH MEMORY (BETTER: LET'S FORGET ABOUT MEMORY)

> The excesses committed in the name of the duty of memory would suggest adopting a duty of forgetting: the formula may displease some, but it imposes itself. Think of Borges's unfortunate hero who could not forget and therefore lived in a hell, unable to erase anything of the chaos that invaded his poor head. The same goes for a human group: by not wanting to forget anything, we expose ourselves to the danger of confusing the living present with a false hallucinatory present that parasitizes present reality for the sake of an obsession with past offenses.
> —Daniel Lindenberg, *Figures d'Israël*

Remembrance Day

When I was a teacher at the Aldini Valeriani night school for adults, in the city of Bologna, every year I dedicated a lot of time to preparing for Remembrance Day.

I read a few pages of Primo Levi, I retraced the events that led to the emergence of German Nazism and explained the meaning of the Shoah in the modern history of Europe.

Once upon a time I asked the students to write an essay on this topic, and a student named Claude completed it in a surprising way. Claude, a Senegalese boy, studious but rather taciturn, wrote that he did not understand why every year the suffering of the Jews is remembered, while there is not a day dedicated to remembering the immense and prolonged suffering of Africans from the slave trade and slavery.

The following day, I devoted the entire next lesson to Claude's essay. I said that, in fact, European memory focuses on an event that, although of enormous importance, is not the only Holocaust in history.

I talked about the great waves of racist extermination. I spoke of the extermination of four-fifths of the Indigenous population of South America by Spanish colonizers. I spoke of the genocide of the Indigenous peoples of North America, and of the extermination of ten million people in the Congo by the Belgian King Leopold II. I spoke of the fact that the English colonizers of the Australian continent, until seventy years ago, could legally shoot and kill Aboriginal Australians.

I concluded by saying that remembering the Holocaust of the Jews also means renewing the memory of all those on every continent who suffered the violence of the exterminating race—white, Christian, and Western.

Remembering the Holocaust means honoring the memory of all those who were victims of genocide. If today I were still teaching in that school for adult, mostly foreign students, as I did until ten years ago, I think I would tell them that after the genocide in Gaza, anyone who intends to celebrate (as is right to do) Remembrance Day must remember that Hitler is but one of the many exterminators of whom modern history is full, and that Netanyahu is an anti-Semite like Hitler was.

In his *Discourse on Colonialism* of 1951, Aimé Césaire writes: "What [the European] cannot forgive Hitler for is not *the crime* in itself, *the crime against man*, it is not *the humiliation of man as such*, it is the crime against the white man, the humiliation of the white man, and the fact that he applied to Europe colonialist procedures which until then had been reserved exclusively for the Arabs of Algeria, the 'coolies' of India, and the 'niggers' of Africa."[1]

Now I'm retired, and I no longer teach, but if today I found myself in front of some kids sitting on school desks, I wouldn't do what I've done so many times in the past. I would not comply with ministerial orders relating to Remembrance Day.

I would say that Remembrance Day is a Western imposture, I would say that six million Jews killed by Nazism have the same value as the we-don't-know-how-many millions of Africans killed, deported, and raped by white Portuguese, English, and American slave owners.

They have the same value as the millions of Palestinians that Israel has driven out, plundered, humiliated, imprisoned, tortured, and exterminated.

They have the same value as the Africans killed by the soldiers in the service of Leopold II, king of Belgium, who according to Mark Twain were ten million, and to whom no one has dedicated a Memorial Museum.

Could Things Have Turned Out Differently?

It is legitimate to ask this question: Could the state desired by the Zionists, authorized by the English colonialists, protected by the American imperialists, armed and financed by the Westerners to dominate the region from which the oil comes, could a state born with a massacre and supported by permanent armed threat have turned out differently?

Could the occupier state have evolved in a direction different from racism, supremacism, fundamentalism—given the predictable hostility of two billion surrounding Muslims?

No, a different evolution was impossible, from the beginning.

It is difficult to believe that the British and the Americans, chiefly responsible (along with the German Nazis, of course) for that deportation of the Jews in the name of a return to the Promised Land, did not know that they were exposing the Jews to a very harsh circumstance, destined to evolve over time toward a new Holocaust.

Israel enjoys undisputed military superiority, but time is not working in its favor.

Could it have turned out differently, or was Israel's evolution inscribed in its violent birth? Could Zionism have evolved in a peaceful direction, or was the hostility with which the occupiers were surrounded from the beginning destined to force Israel to become what it has become?

It couldn't have turned out differently, and a group of twenty-eight Jewish intellectuals who sent a letter to *The New York Times* on December 2, 1948, were aware of the danger.

These intellectuals denounced the fascist direction imposed by Menachem Begin on the nature of the Israeli state. They knew that the Zionist decision to impose the presence of the State of Israel in the Middle East could only evolve badly.

Among these intellectuals were Hannah Arendt and Albert Einstein, and they can hardly be accused of anti-Semitism.

Let's read their letter, because it says everything we could repeat today about the congenital fascism of the Zionist state.

> TO THE EDITOR OF *THE NEW YORK TIMES*:
>
> Among the most disturbing political phenomena of our times is the emergence in the newly created state of Israel of the "Freedom Party" (Tnuat Haherut), a political party closely akin in its organization, methods, political philosophy and social

appeal to the Nazi and Fascist parties. It was formed out of the membership and following of the former Irgun Zvai Leumi, a terrorist, right-wing, chauvinist organization in Palestine.

The current visit of Menachen Begin, leader of this party, to the United States is obviously calculated to give the impression of American support for his party in the coming Israeli elections, and to cement political ties with conservative Zionist elements in the United States. Several Americans of national repute have lent their names to welcome his visit. It is inconceivable that those who oppose fascism throughout the world, if correctly informed as to Mr. Begin's political record and perspectives, could add their names and support to the movement he represents.

Before irreparable damage is done by way of financial contributions, public manifestations in Begin's behalf, and the creation in Palestine of the impression that a large segment of America supports Fascist elements in Israel, the American public must be informed as to the record and objectives of Mr. Begin and his movement.

The public avowals of Begin's party are no guide whatever to its actual character. Today they speak of freedom, democracy and anti-imperialism, whereas until recently they openly preached the doctrine of the Fascist state. It is in its actions that the terrorist party betrays its real character; from its past actions we can judge what it may be expected to do in the future.

Attack on Arab Village

A shocking example was their behavior in the Arab village of Deir Yassin. This village, off the main roads and surrounded by Jewish lands, had taken no part in the war, and had even fought off Arab bands who wanted to use the village as their base. On April 9 (*THE NEW YORK TIMES*), terrorist bands attacked this peaceful village, which was not a military objective in the fighting, killed most of its inhabitants—240 men, women and children—and kept a few of them alive to parade as captives through the streets of Jerusalem. Most of the Jewish community was horrified at the deed, and the Jewish Agency sent a telegram of apology to King Abdullah of Trans-Jordan. But the terrorists, far from being ashamed of their act, were proud of this massacre, publicized it widely, and invited all the foreign correspondents present in the country to view the heaped corpses and the general havoc at Deir Yassin.

The Deir Yassin incident exemplifies the character and actions of the Freedom Party.

Within the Jewish community they have preached an admixture of ultra-nationalism, religious mysticism, and racial superiority. Like other Fascist parties they have been used to break strikes, and have themselves pressed for the destruction of free trade unions. In their stead they have proposed corporate unions on the Italian Fascist model.

During the last years of sporadic anti-British violence, the IZL and Stern groups inaugurated a reign of terror in the Palestine Jewish community. Teachers were beaten up for speaking against them, adults were shot for not letting their children join them. By gangster methods, beatings, window-smashing, and wide-spread robberies, the terrorists intimidated the population and exacted a heavy tribute.

The people of the Freedom Party have had no part in the constructive achievements in Palestine. They have reclaimed no land, built no settlements, and only detracted from the Jewish defense activity. Their much-publicized immigration endeavors were minute, and devoted mainly to bringing in Fascist compatriots.

Discrepancies Seen

The discrepancies between the bold claims now being made by Begin and his party, and their record of past performance in Palestine bear the imprint of no ordinary political party. This is the unmistakable stamp of a Fascist party for whom terrorism (against Jews, Arabs, and British alike), and misrepresentation are means, and a "Leader State" is the goal.

In the light of the foregoing considerations, it is imperative that the truth about Mr. Begin and his movement be made known in this country. It is all the more tragic that the top leadership of American Zionism has refused to campaign against Begin's efforts, or even to expose to its own constituents the dangers to Israel from support to Begin.

The undersigned therefore take this means of

publicly presenting a few salient facts concerning Begin and his party; and of urging all concerned not to support this latest manifestation of fascism.

ISIDORE ABRAMOWITZ, HANNAH ARENDT, ABRAHAM BRICK, RABBI JESSURUN CARDOZO, ALBERT EINSTEIN, HERMAN EISEN, M. D., HAYIM FINEMAN, M. GALLEN, M. D., H. H. HARRIS, ZELIG S. HARRIS, SIDNEY HOOK, FRED KARUSH, BRURIA KAUFMAN, IRMA L. LINDHEIM, NACHMAN MAJSEL, SEYMOUR MELMAN, MYER D. MENDELSON, M. D., HARRY M. ORLINSKY, SAMUEL PITLICK, FRITZ ROHRLICH, LOUIS P. ROCKER, RUTH SAGER, ITZHAK SANKOWSKY, I. J. SCHOENBERG, SAMUEL SHUMAN, M. ZNGER, IRMA WOLPE, STEFAN WOLPE.[2]

A Tale of Love and Darkness, but Above All Darkness

Shortly before his death, Amos Oz gave a talk at the annual international conference of the Institute for National Security Studies.

I have been a reader of Oz for a long time, and I believe that books like *A Tale of Love and Darkness* and *Judas* gave me the ability to reflect on the fundamental questions of Jewish identity, and identity in general.

Identity as a problem, as an illusory construction and as a trap.

Rightly or wrongly, I have learned to consider Amos Oz's work an expression of the internationalist vocation of European Jewry.

In *A Tale of Love and Darkness*, Oz writes:

> My Uncle David ... was a confirmed European, at a time when, it seems, no one else in Europe was, apart from the members of my family and other Jews like them. Everyone else turns out to have been Pan-Slavic, Pan-Germanic, or simply Latvian, Bulgarian, Irish, or Slovak patriots. The only Europeans in the whole of Europe in the 1920s and 1930s were the Jews. My father always used to say: In Czechoslovakia there are three nations, the Czechs, the Slovaks, and the Czecho-Slovaks, i.e., the Jews; in Yugoslavia there are Serbs, Croats, Slovenes, and Montenegrines, but, even there, there lives a group of unmistakable Yugoslavs; and even in Stalin's empire there are Russians, there are Ukrainians, and there are Uzbeks and Chukchis and Tatars, and among them are our brethren, the only real members of a *Soviet* nation.
>
> Europe has now changed completely, and is full of Europeans from wall to wall. Incidentally, the graffiti in Europe have also changed from wall to wall. When my father was a young man in Vilna, every wall in Europe said, "Jews go home to Palestine." Fifty years later, when he went back to Europe on a visit, the walls all screamed, "Jews get out of Palestine."[3]

Actually, it is not the Jews who wanted to return to Palestine. It is the European (not only German) Nazis who pushed them to leave. And the Zionists, together with the English government, since the Balfour declaration of

1917, have been preparing the trap into which the Jews fell. That trap is called Israel.

Like many other European Jews, the writer's parents abandoned Europe to take refuge in Palestine, in the years when the Zionist project seemed poised to be realized peacefully.

In the era that Oz is talking about, there seemed to be room for a solidarity-based, egalitarian, and internationalist conscience. But because nationalism dominated European politics, the Jews, too, had to identify themselves as a people, as a nation, if they wanted to survive. He writes: "In those days all the Poles were drunk on Polishness, the Ukrainians were drunk on Ukrainianness, not to mention the Germans, the Czechs, all of them, even the Slovaks, the Lithuanians, and the Latvians, and there was no place for us in that carnival, we didn't belong and we weren't wanted. Small wonder that we too wanted to be a nation, like the rest of them. What alternative had they left us?"[4]

We know what happened in the end: after having exterminated them, the Europeans spewed out the Jewish community, which was also the most profoundly European, because it most fully embodied the values of rationalism and law. Precisely because the Jews did not have an ancestral relationship with the European land, their Europeanism was founded on reason and law, not on ethnic identity.

Eventually, the Shoah forced Jews to desire belonging as a defense against racism, and to undertake the path toward national identity, and toward the negation of universalism in the name of the ethnic state. Zionism embodies this understandable and catastrophic passage.

On the night that the foundation of the State of Israel is sanctioned at the United Nations, the father of the narrator of *A Tale of Love and Darkness* says to his son: "From now on, from the moment we have our own state, you will never be bullied just because you are a Jew and because Jews are so-and-sos. Not that. Never again. From tonight that's finished here. Forever."[5]

Unfortunately, as we know, Oz's father was mistaken: the creation of the State of Israel set in motion an endless chain of suffering and revenge.

After 1947, nationalism and the Nakba made peaceful coexistence between Arabs and Jews impossible. On the one hand, the Arab political entities that emerged from the disintegration of the Ottoman Empire had revived the model of European nationalism and did not peacefully welcome the Jews onto their territory. On the other, the Jews claimed the right to establish a nation-state in a territory that did not belong to them and was hostile to them.

Since 1948, young Israelis have been forced to fight an interminable war, and young Palestinians have been forced to live in refugee camps where they can do nothing but hate the occupiers and prepare for rebellion: intifada.

In these conditions, it was inevitable that the Israeli political balance would shift toward nationalism, up to the current coalition between fascists and Orthodox

Israelis that has transformed Israel into a dangerous monster first of all for the Jews.

In the centuries of the diaspora, universalism had been the *forma mentis* of Jewish intellectuality, but when the Jews founded their own state and were called to identify themselves territorially, an effect of identification of the "other" was produced: the Palestinian. Many young Israelis were forced to fight a war they hated, for a nationalistic ideal they did not believe in.

> One winter evening I happened to be on night duty with Efraim Avneri. … I asked Ephraim if he had ever, in the War of Independence or during the troubles in the 1930s, shot and killed one of those murderers.
>
> I could not see Ephraim's face in the dark, but there was a certain subversive irony, a strange sarcastic sadness in his voice as he replied, after a short pensive silence:
>
> "Murderers? What d'you expect from them? From their point of view, we are aliens from outer space who have landed and trespassed on their land, gradually taken over parts of it, and while we promise them that we've come here to lavish all sorts of goodies on them … we've craftily grabbed more and more of their land. Vell, what did you think? That they should thank us? That they should come out to greet us with drums and cymbals? That they should respectfully hand over the keys to the whole land just because our ancestors lived here once? Is it any wonder they've taken up arms against us? And

now that we've inflicted a crushing defeat on them and hundreds of thousands of them are living in refugee camps—what, d'you expect them to celebrate with us and wish us luck?"

... I was so stunned that I asked him sarcastically:

"In that case, what are you doing here with your gun? Why don't you emigrate? Or take your gun and go fight on their side?"

I could hear his sad smile in the dark:

"Their side? But their side doesn't want me. Nowhere in the world wants me. Nobody in the world wants me. That's the whole point. It seems there are too many of my kind in every country. That's the only reason I'm here. That's the only reason I'm carrying a gun, so they won't kick me out of here the way they kicked me out of everywhere else. But you won't find me using the word "murderers" about Arabs who've lost their villages. At least, not easily. About Nazi, yes. About Stalin, also. And about whoever steals other people's land."[6]

Pages like this convinced me that Amos Oz understood the contradiction of being Israeli, as they seemed to express the desire for peace between different peoples: the opposite of Zionism.

Judas the Internationalist

Published in 2014, Amos Oz's novel *Judas* tells the story of a young researcher who studies the historical figure of Judas Iscariot—identified by the Christian as the traitor par excellence, and as the symbol of Jewish wickedness.

Not reducible to national identity, betrayal is the meaning of modern rationality and its historical figure: the intellectual. The intellectual, the Jewish figure par excellence, is the one who betrays national identity in the name of the universality of reason. This is why fascism is fundamentally anti-intellectual.

As for the image of the betrayer, Oz writes some lines in *Contro il fanatismo* (*How to Cure a Fanatic*): "My perception is that in the conflict between Israeli and Palestinian Arabs, there are no good and bad guys. There is a tragedy: the conflict between one right and another. I have repeated these words so many times that I have earned the title of certified traitor in the eyes of many Israeli citizens."[7]

The word *betrayal* can be translated as "internationalism," because this political culture, which had some fortune in the twentieth century, means radical rejection of the nation, rejection of the logic of belonging and therefore rejection of war. "Desertion" is another way to translate *betrayal* and *internationalism*.

The character of Abravanel, a cultured and polyglot Jew who appears in *Judas*, has no sympathy for the State of Israel, because he considers the very idea of the nation-state to be evidence of cultural backwardness. How can modern man accept such a denial of the ethical universalism that from Kant onward should be the foundation of politics?

> Abravanel was never impressed by nationalism. At all. Anywhere. He was totally unimpressed by a world divided into hundreds of nation-states, like rows and rows of separate cages in a zoo. He didn't know Yiddish—he spoke Hebrew and Arabic, he spoke Ladino, English, French, Turkish, and Greek—but to all the states in the world he applied a Yiddish expression: *goyim naches*. Gentiles' delight. Statehood seemed to him a childish and outdated concept.[8]

An internationalist, as I consider myself, cannot accept the "two peoples, two states" agenda that is (was) the official belief of the international community. I have always been convinced that this formula is based on a principle that is unacceptable, because it implies that political entities (such as the state) are based on ethnic identity or religious belonging.

Franco Piperno was a leader of the Italian organization Potere Operaio. He was a communist and a Jew. I remember that he said one day, at a meeting on the Israeli-Palestine conflict, that the nation-state is never the solution. It is always the problem.

And he added that two states could not offer a peaceful coexistence to those people who inhabited the land of Israel, or Palestine, which are the same place.

When the Europeans got rid of the Jews, expelling them toward the Middle Eastern desert, the conditions of an infinite tragedy were established: the poisoned fruit of the victory of nationalism against internationalism.

Atalia, the wife of a young Israeli killed during a firefight with the Arabs in the novel, knows this well.

> Atalia eyed him slantwise from the couch … and seemed to spit her words:
>
> "You wanted a state. You wanted independence. Flags and uniforms and banknotes and drums and trumpets. You shed rivers of innocent blood. You sacrificed an entire generation. You drove hundreds of thousands of Arabs out of their homes. You sent shiploads of Holocaust survivors straight from the quayside to the battlefield. All so that there would be a Jewish state here. And look what you've got."[9]

I share from the bottom of my heart the contempt that Atalia expresses for the nation-state. And it seems to me that Amos Oz's heart felt the same feeling when he wrote these pages.

This is why when I read the writer's last speech, I felt some unease, as if not recognizing the voice of a friend.

Giving this address in 2018, Oz looked different from the person whom I knew from reading his novels. Maybe the mistake was mine, maybe I had misunderstood. Maybe in the last period of his life Amos Oz lost all hope in the possibility of a political community based on the coexistence of different cultures, in which rights are based on reason and not on belonging and tradition.

Indeed, in his "last lesson," Oz says: "Do not be fooled by what beautiful souls say about the multiethnic or binational state as the homeland of all its citizens. There is no such thing."[10]

I don't know if I must, begrudgingly, consider myself to be a beautiful soul, but I am convinced that there is no civilization, no moral decency, no peace if you think that the state must correspond to ethnicity, religion, identity. Has Amos Oz really always meant what he says in his last speech? Has he really always identified with ugly souls?

In this text, Oz accuses those who speak of "free Palestine" of being affected by a sort of pathological "homesickness."[11]

"You are sick," he recalls having once told a Palestinian intellectual who wanted to go back to his native village occupied by the colonists. "You are sick and I have a diagnosis for your sickness: you suffer from 'returnism.' You want to find in space something that has been lost in time."[12]

I am not a fanatic of memory, and I recognize that a policy cannot be based on nostalgia for what was ours in the past, but something rings false in this invitation to emancipate ourselves from the past, because it comes from a Jew who returns to a land that his ancestors inhabited two thousand years ago. How can he laugh at a man who misses the house his parents lived in?

Oz himself, moments later, wonders if he too, and his family, his parents who returned to Israel two thousand years after leaving, are not suffering from "returnism." But he absolves himself and his fellow Israelis from this accusation.

With some uneasiness and embarrassment, I read these words from one of my favorite writers, and I think of those from another, whose name is Mahmoud Darwish: "You [Israelis] have caused our exile, we haven't caused yours."[13]

The fanaticism that has spread like a weed in contemporary Israeli society is not only the fruit of religious faith. It is bringing together laypeople and believers in a shared obsession with the defense of identity …

Their common belief is this: Israel cannot exist except as a Jewish homeland. If others want to live in Israel as minorities, they must adapt and be subjected to the supremacy of the Jews.

A corollary necessarily follows this postulate: there can be no other homeland than Israel for the Jews.

To the founder of so-called Revisionist Zionism, Vladimir Jabotinsky, who in opposition to David Ben-Gurion pursued the birth of an exclusively Jewish state, is attributed a recommendation that has remained proverbial: "Eliminate the Diaspora, or the Diaspora will surely eliminate you."[14]

Now, after the Gaza genocide, that recommendation must be reconsidered. The Israeli citizens, as divided as they are on many issues, seem to agree on the necessity of extermination, but the diaspora is much more divided.

A significant part of the Jews who live in the United States share the views of the Israeli right wing, up to the point of marching together with the evangelical racists of the MAGA coalition.

But we have seen a crowd of New York Jews unfurling a "Palestinians should be free" banner at the Statue of Liberty, while wearing t-shirts saying "Not in our name."[15] We have seen the participation of many young Jewish students in the university protests against the genocide.

In an interview given to the Italian newspaper *la Repubblica* a few years ago, Netanyahu articulated the absolutely cynical line of moral and political reasoning that has guided Israel over the last twenty years.

"History is impartial and unforgiving," he said. "It does not favour the virtuous, nor who is morally superior. ... If we want to protect our values, our rights, our freedoms, we must be strong. The lesson from the past is that moral superiority does not guarantee the survival of our civilisation."[16]

These words are unequivocal. *In history, there is no space for the respect of the other; if we want to survive, we must ignore pity and human feelings. Moral superiority does not guarantee the survival of our civilization.*

But I wonder: What kind of civilization is this, if it is dependent on force, on military superiority, on extermination?

The question that I cannot avoid asking myself is this: Was it necessary to establish a nation-state, to retrace the past history of Europe that was founded on war, oppression, the domination of the strongest, which lasts until the oppressed becomes stronger than the oppressor?

Zeev Sternhell said many times that particularism and antirationalism are today once again at the basis of the threat of world war.

Here we are: on the edge of this abyss, and it's hard to say how we can avoid it. Wasn't it possible to experience a form of egalitarian coexistence with those who inhabited that territory? Idle questions, I tell myself.

Internationalism has not had the strength to impose itself, neither in Palestine nor elsewhere. Therefore violence is the only way for people to survive: *We need to equip ourselves with a nation-state, an army, and the cynicism necessary to impose the only law that counts, which is the law of ferocity.*

Today the law of ferocity allows the Israeli to exterminate Palestinians. But tomorrow?

Who will be the exterminator tomorrow, who the exterminated?

Should we bow our heads before the lesson of history?

Or is it necessary to abandon history, to leave this nightmare without imagination, this chain of revenge where *friendship* is a word for the deluded poor?

Even if we don't know how desertion is possible, nor what road leads out of this litany of horror, only outside of historical repetition can we find humanity.

Memory and Power

We have been trained to believe that memory is a good thing.

In any case, humans remember, whether they want to or not.

At the risk of appearing silly, however, I ask myself: Do we really need to remember? Is the ritual of revisiting the past—past pain, violence suffered—really useful?

The cult of memory is so profound, respected, indisputable that it can only be questioned for fun.

Nevertheless, I dare to say it: memory has always functioned as a guarantee of the eternal continuation of hatred.

The ritualization of memory functions as a reinforcement of identity, but also as a promise of revenge.

Milan Kundera writes: "The struggle of man against power is the struggle of memory against forgetting."[17]

I believe exactly the opposite.

Power is the inescapable authoritarian hierarchical organization of memory, it is the compulsion to repeat, the cult of roots, the aggressive and resentful cult of imaginary homelands, the accumulation of value, the memory of past work.

The struggle to distance ourselves from power (and perhaps to destroy it) only makes sense if it is a liberation from memory, from all memories.

What do we need to remember? The vast violence, the countless injustices we have suffered? The first effect of this (indelible) memory is paralysis, fear. The second effect is resentment, the desire for revenge.

If we want to become different, however, from what we have been in the past, we need to free ourselves from the trace that submission has left in our soul. We need to abandon every identity, every memory of what we have been and what we have suffered. Only by deserting memory, history, and truth can we find some (tiny) space for joy.

Nationalism, oppression, war have their origins in the memory of a past. And memory is deceptive, as Kundera himself says. Like a taffeta jacket, memory changes and evolves, because by moving away from it, we change perspective, and therefore we see something from the past that we did not see until a moment before, or we erase something from the past that we no longer feel like remembering.

Generally, memory turns into resentment, then evolves into revenge. Therefore memory can be the enemy of friendship.

Chaim Weizmann was once asked the question: What gives you the right to the territory of Palestine? He replied: "Memory is right."[18] *Memory is a right*. Or, also: *Memory is always right, it doesn't make mistakes*.

It is not true. Chaim Weizmann lied, or rather said something that didn't make sense. Memory does not confer any rights and does not mean anything ethically or legally relevant. And above all, memory can make mistakes—it often makes mistakes. I would almost say that memory *always* makes mistakes, because it reconstructs past events according to criteria that did not exist in the past.

Memory is simply a fiction of a return from the past. A past that is deformed, however, as Kundera says very well.

Nonetheless, memory is the foundation of the nation: a deceptive, fictitious foundation, continually redefined because, as Kundera says, memory changes depending on each new context. In fact, memory is not enough to found a nation; in addition to memory, war is needed.

Memory is the source of hatred and war.

The Western powers recognized, albeit with some delay, the validity of Weizmann's unfounded request. After the Second World War, after the Shoah, we witnessed the birth of a country that, in the name of the memory, claimed its right to return to a land from which it believed it was expelled two thousand years ago, and claimed the right to exercise violence against the Arab-Palestinian population.

The principle "a land without a people for a people without a land" was then formulated.

But this was a false principle, because there was a people in that land. So much so that the birth of the State of Israel coincided with the massacre of tens of thousands of people and with the beginning of a process of persecution and deportation that continues today, seventy-five years later.

From the beginning, the State of Israel has been based on a genocidal principle. Precisely because it was based on the false assumption that the land promised by a highly hypothetical god was "a land without a people," from that moment on it was necessary to eliminate any evidence of the fact that that people existed.

It was necessary to exterminate those people who proved the falsity of the assumption on which the State of Israel is based. Today, two or three generations later, the Zionists have become the most advanced department of racism in the world.

Bernard-Henri Lévy and Giuliano Ferrara, among others, flaunt their Judaism as if this gives them the right to any arrogance. Yet they are not at all victims, but grandchildren or great-grandchildren of the victims.

After all, it is well known that victims usually prefer not to remember, while the great-grandchildren of the victims continually remind themselves and everyone else that they are victims and therefore are absolved in principle of any crime they may commit.

These heirs of the victims do not want peace, they just want to become executioners themselves, as if this would restore justice. They are incapable of forgetting because forgetting is not convenient for them: they would lose their privilege.

The Gaze of the Persecutor as a Source of Memory

> As the sixteenth century progressed, ... conformity [to the old religion] became exceptional. A new generation grew up, with no first-hand acquaintance of official Judaism, no knowledge of the traditional language of prayer, and no literature for their guidance. All that they had to go upon was oral tradition and the authority of the Jewish Scriptures, which remained accessible to them in the Latin version. To this we may perhaps add the edicts and fulminations of the Inquisition itself,

> which in certain cases demonstrably served to indicate to those wavering in their faith what they should do, instead of the practices which they should avoid.[19]

When memory is besieged by persecution, only the gaze of the persecutor allows the persecuted to recognize themselves.

In this way identity is built, a disease of memory: through the assumption of the gaze of others as a definition of the self.

Sometimes memory can become overwhelming, as happens in "Funes the Memorious" by Borges. Funes is unable to forget, and is oppressed by an excess of memories that finally kills him.

Sometimes we lose the memory of the idiom, we lose the meaning of the signs, as happens to the inhabitants of Macondo that García Márquez talks about in *One Hundred Years of Solitude*.

The hypermnemonic Funes remembers every detail of his past and every experience, even irrelevant ones, so that memory overload prevents him from living and thinking. The inhabitants of Macondo are losing their memory of what words mean, and how things are called, so they attach a tag with a written name on every object. But in the end, even the memory of the meaning of these signs vanishes.

At that point, when memory has faded, what remains?

What remains is the gaze of the persecutor who tells you who you are, who forces you to be what he sees.

Frankly speaking, I believe that we would all be happier if we were capable of forgetting. But three thousand years of hatred, war, and the Bible have proven that we are not capable of it. We are not capable of forgetting the evil we have received; therefore memory obsesses us and pushes us to repeat it, so that we inflict against those who are weaker the violence that we suffered from those who were stronger.

Therefore, since oblivion is not granted to us, memory is welcome.

But at least let memory be respectful of the truth.

The first truth we remember is that the Jews were victims of immense violence by Hitler's Nazi regime and by all European peoples—the French, the Poles, the Italians, the Romanians, the Ukrainians—who largely supported the persecution of the Jews.

The second truth is that the Holocaust is just one of many genocides through which white supremacy has subjugated the peoples of the world for centuries, forcing them to suffer colonial exploitation.

The third truth is that the State of Israel is continuing the chain of crimes and revenge that is late modern history. The violence to which the Jews were subjected in the 1940s is the same violence to which the colonized peoples of Asia, Africa, and America were subjected at different times.

The genocidal campaign taking place in Gaza brutally redefines the very meaning of our memory of the past.

Israel's racist and colonialist violence is nothing new; it began in 1948 with the forced deportation of seven hundred thousand Palestinians, and continued with the creation of an apartheid regime, with the continuous humiliation of the Palestinians by Israeli troops, with the systematic destruction of Palestinian homes in the West Bank, with the multiplication of armed colonial settlements that put the West Bank under military control. Since 2005, Gaza has been a concentration camp from which it is impossible to escape and in which daily life is made impossible by continuous aggression.

In recent years, we had believed that the issue was resolved with the definitive humiliation of the Palestinians, but the atrocious revenge of October 7 forced everyone to understand that this was not the case.

After that date, Israel's response became so similar to a genocide that no one in the world can any longer ignore what many did not know until October 7: for seventy-five years, Palestinians have been subjected to deportation, discrimination, ethnic internment in extermination camps, random killings and targeted killings.

In Europe it is forbidden to tell these truths that no historian can deny. Those who were responsible for the extermination of the Jewish people—that is, the European peoples—became supporters of Israeli colonization in Palestine after the defeat of Hitler's Germany. Those Europeans who were the most anti-Semitic in the past, those who are the most openly fascist in the present: those are today the most inflexible supporters of national Zionism.

In Germany, the official truth of the state is based on the premise that Israel's actions are unquestionable. But in the name of this impossibility of judging the actions of Israel (which claims to be the state of the Jews), the German state has criminally prosecuted, or expelled, Jewish intellectuals who have criticized Israel in the name of universal values, in the name of the defense of human life.

The political and cultural forces that were the most openly anti-Semitic and participated in the genocide of the Jews are today Israel's staunchest supporters. Precisely because they collaborated with Nazism, they support Israel's policies toward the Palestinians.

We must say these things on Remembrance Day; otherwise, we will repeat rhetorical, hypocritical, and false words.

Beyond Memory

While we exercise our memory, however, it would be appropriate to also exercise our imagination and anticipation of the future.

Israeli aggression has opened an abyss between colonialism and the colonized world.

In an article published on January 17, 2024, Saul J. Takahashi, a professor at the University of Osaka, asserts that the event called Gaza will be the grave of Western hegemony in the world: "By supporting Israel's atrocities in Gaza, the West has shredded what remains of its credibility and brought the 'rules-based' world order it purports to lead to the point of no return."[20]

I believe Takahashi is right: Israel is perceived throughout the world as the outpost of Western colonialism. A part of the Jewish community, especially in the diaspora, is today perfectly aware of the unacceptability of Israeli lies. *Israelism*, the documentary by Erin Axelman and Sam Eilertsen, two Jewish filmmakers, shows the mixture of supremacism and ethno-religious fanaticism that has taken shape in Israeli culture and in US racist-Trumpist evangelism. And it shows how the fusion between secular colonialism and religious fundamentalism has produced effects of aggression and systematic oppression.

Gaza has become the nucleus of an ethical revolt of global proportions: the white world defends itself belligerently in defense of genocidal Zionism, but finds itself increasingly isolated, besieged by the growing hatred of the Global South and also by the revolt of young people—first and foremost, by the revolt of American Jewish students.

Colonialism survived the anticolonial struggles of the twentieth century and today presents itself as a wounded beast ready to do anything to avoid extinction.

We know that "ready for anything" means *ready for genocide.*

The disintegration of white civilization and genocide stand together in the backdrop of the advancing century.

4

DISINTEGRATION

Disintegration is the order of the day throughout the West. The population of every Western country, such as that of the United States, not to mention that of Israel, is irreconcilably divided around alternatives that are largely false, such as the alternative between liberal democracy and authoritarian tyranny. There is no liberal democracy, and it is reductive to define the power of Putin or Trump as authoritarian tyranny. Both forms are rather the political (i.e., spectacular) manifestation of the increasingly inescapable power of the financial system and the techno-military system. But if the alternative between liberal democracy and authoritarian tyranny is false, disintegration is real.

For now it is not a question of political disintegration but rather of a psychic and cultural disintegration. Political disintegration is bound to follow.

The impotence of political will in governing environmental devastation, as well as financial flows, and in containing the resulting impoverishment, has produced an effect of humiliation and withdrawal in the white mind.

In order to deny our impotence, sometimes we are led to blame others: immigrants, foreigners, sexual deviants, whomever.

Aging and the loss of psychosexual energy have magnified the fear of an invasion of young foreigners.

The collapse of the Protestant ethic and its replacement by the baroque beliefs of media evangelism has spread a monstrous mass of infantilism and cynicism: Trump's triumph is not (only) a crisis of political democracy, but it also and above all signals the psychotic collapse of a senescent and cognitively crippled population. The conflict between those who believe in authoritarian exorcism and those who believe in democratic exorcism has brought Western societies to a point of irreversible breakdown, because exorcisms do not serve to restore a political order that was once based on social, cultural, and psychic integration.

Psychotic Israel

The United States is the largest and most alarming scene of this disintegration of the Western mind, but Israel is perhaps the place where psychic disintegration will have the most explosive effects.

Israel will only be able to postpone disintegration by prolonging the genocidal war that devastates the existence of millions of Palestinian men and women, but also the minds of millions of Israeli men and women.

In an interview published in October 2024, Anna Foa used the expression "losing one's soul" to describe the dangerous idea, which turns out to be an illusion, that Israel is a democracy that aspires to peace and security.[1]

My belief is that the Israeli soul has always been encumbered by the awareness of an original "sin," of a founding colonialist violence. But the illusion of a peaceful future could exist and be passed down, perhaps, until October 7. Today no one can believe it anymore, and what remains is not only the ferocity of Israel but also the deep weakness, the shame that cannot be removed forever from the conscience, and the awareness of the fact that, despite the genocide, time is not working in this genocidal country's favor.

The Israelis have so far managed not to see what the whole world has seen: the genocide taking place just a few miles from their homes.

The Israelis have managed not to know that the main person responsible for the October 7 massacre was Benjamin Netanyahu, as the Israeli historian Adam Raz has explained in a book titled *The Road to October 7: Benjamin Netanyahu, the Production of the Endless Conflict, and Israel's Moral Degradation*.[2]

The Israelis have managed not to understand that what their soldiers have committed and continue to commit is genocide.

But when the fragile defenses of repression collapse, when the Israelis are forced to realize that every decent person in the world is horrified by what Israel has done, I don't think that Israel will be able to continue to exist.

Israel should never have been born. The British should never have created such a monster, the Americans should never have supported it. But Israel is now destined to rapidly destroy itself, because the horror that the Israelis have sown, and which will end up clouding their minds, is already driving this people toward suicide.

The press does not report the numbers of Israeli soldiers who kill themselves after returning from the front, it does not inform the public about the wave of nervous breakdowns nor about the spread of post-traumatic stress disorder among the young killers of the Israel Defense Forces.

Dahlia Scheindlin, a journalist for the Israeli newspaper *Haaretz*, writes: "Trigger warning … I didn't have one last week when a photo of a girl with half a head appeared on my feed one morning. Her fuzzy pink wrap was almost indistinguishable from the part that was once inside her head, now splayed out around her body. Her face, however, was mostly preserved, her frozen eyes half-closed and yet gazing back at me."[3]

Self-horror is accumulating in the Israeli psyche.

Dahlia Scheindlin also wonders whether soldiers sent to fight in Gaza should refuse military orders: "The issue of the refusal to obey military orders remains one of the most sensitive, toxic subjects in Israel."[4] Perhaps a topic that cannot be discussed?

In the October 24, 2024, issue of *il manifesto*, Sarah Parenzo writes: "Over 12 months of more or less direct exposure to violence, deaths, injuries, hostages, displaced persons, demonstrations, economic and political uncertainty and constant danger, manipulated by institutions which, instead of ferrying the country out of the crisis, only add fuel to the fire, have bent even the nervous systems of the most resilient."[5]

The physical and mental exhaustion of the Israeli torturers brings to mind what Jonathan Littell portrays in his novel *The Kindly Ones*: the state of mental chaos, nausea, self-horror experienced by the SS who for months and years have killed, tortured, massacred … and finally are no longer able to recognize their own faces in the mirror.[6]

The horror that the IDF exterminators instill in every person with human feelings cannot fail to act as a factor of deep disintegration in those who have carried out acts that have made them identical to the Nazi exterminators.

The psychotic reverse side of identification with the oppressor will manifest itself in many cases as self-hatred.

From this point of view, the atrocious trap set by Hamas was sprung perfectly: the hostage crisis has created a wound that will never heal.

The resentment toward Netanyahu, who has done everything possible to prolong the war, as if he doesn't care at all about saving the hostages, is destined to have explosive political effects when sooner or later the conclusions are drawn and the cynical conduct of the massacre is called to account.

It is very likely that the responsibility of the Israeli leadership for the October 7 massacre will emerge; what Adam Raz writes cannot remain relegated to the conscience of a few.

What will happen when everyone is forced to know that the executioner Netanyahu has those twelve hundred deaths on his conscience?

Israeli society is destined to disintegrate under the weight of self-horror, but not only because of this.

The economy has been collapsing for some time, and this is not a temporary situation, because those who have careers that allow them to find work outside the country are leaving. The doctors are leaving. Entrepreneurs are fleeing.

How many intellectuals worthy of the title will be able to remain in a country that stands out for its ferocity and fanaticism? Within Israel there is a courageous minority that continues to carry out its reporting and critique, as demonstrated by intellectually excellent publications such as *+972 Magazine* and the *Haaretz* newspaper. But at the end of November 2024, the government of Israel (the only democracy in the Middle East, right?) has begun to tighten the noose around *Haaretz*'s neck, banning advertising funding for this newspaper that has no intention of bowing to the fascism of the only democracy in the Middle East.

What will remain then?

What will remain are the religious fanatics and those who came to Israel to take over other people's land, the settlers whom Smotrich armed with one hundred thousand machine guns.

They too, with their beautiful machine guns and their beautiful hands stained with the blood of the children of the West Bank, will sooner or later have to understand it: Israel is surrounded by the hatred of two billion Muslims, it is a country in which every car that passes on the street could suddenly turn to kill those who are waiting at the bus stop.

Under these conditions, what can stop the disintegration of this country that should never have existed?

It is true that the jackals of international finance have begun to invest in the reconstruction of Gaza, after the genocide and deportation.

"I am incredibly optimistic about Israel's tech economy and the broader economy," Shaun Maguire, a partner at Sequoia Capital, one of the largest venture capital funds in the world, said in a recent interview with the financial newspaper *Globes*.[7]

It is true that in the fourth quarter of 2024, while the corpses accumulate above and below the rubble, there is a growth of 3.4 percentage points in the gross domestic product of the genocidal country.

On the other hand, however, many multinational companies have abandoned the genocidal country. China is terminating contracts for the supply of electronic components for electric cars, because the tricky joke of explosive pagers suggests that there is no point in putting ourselves in the hands of high-tech professional assassins. Tourism is over, and it is hard to imagine how it can be reborn.

On May 28, 2024, 130 leading Israeli economists wrote to their government that the country has entered a downward spiral toward its collapse.

The signatories of this letter, reported by the *Globes*, included Prof. Eitan Sheshinski, Prof. Manuel Trajtenberg, Prof. Avi Ben-Bassat, Prof. Danny Ben David, Dr. Michael Sarel, Prof. Momi Dahan, Prof. Itai Ater, Prof. Omer Moav, Prof. Leo Leiderman, Prof. Amir Barnea, Prof. Yossi Spiegel, and former senior government officials such as David Brodet, Keren Terner, Shaul Meridor, Prof. Udi Nisan, Prof. Michel Strawczynski, and Roni Hizkiyahu.[8]

The Disintegration of the Greatest Power of All Time

How to destroy the greatest military power of all time?

An interesting question, which no one had been able to answer until two planes led by Osama bin Laden's emissaries appeared in the sky over New York.

In its brutality, that attack was a masterpiece of strategy, and began the process that today reaches its turning point. The American leadership did exactly what bin Laden had hoped, wanted, and desired. A less intellectually gifted president followed the instructions of his deputy, who was only interested in making profits for his companies offering war services. This was how the United States began the process that led them to 2021, when Biden mumbled in front of the cameras meaningless sentences and plain lies in order to reassure the world about what was happening in Kabul.

While Biden was mumbling, gigantic fights broke out at the airport, people climbed onto the sides of departing planes, and in the stampede a bomb explosion killed more than two hundred people.

In the following years, Biden had the idea of pushing the Ukrainians to war.

Forgetting the elementary principle that inspires every empire that wants to survive—divide and conquer—Biden obtained the predictable result of bringing Russia and China closer together in a military alliance. Two and a half years later, Ukraine is in a disastrous state and its final defeat appears inevitable, while the anti-Western front has grown economically, diplomatically, and militarily.

At this juncture came the presidential brawl between two old men, then Biden's resignation, the brief appearance of Kamala Harris, and finally the triumph of the man who promises to give the furious Americans back their dominance: America *über alles*.

But Trump's election can only accelerate the disintegration.

A gang of mafiosi, racists, and rapists in the White House will hardly be able to coexist with the deep state apparatus—that is, with a rival gang of rapists, racists, and mafiosi.

How will the military apparatus be able to coexist for very long with a president who proposes the destruction of the Atlantic Alliance?

How will the inhabitants of the East and West coasts be able to live with the authoritarian offensive?

How will the mass deportation of immigrants be able to coexist with an economy that is largely based on the low wages of undocumented workers?

Is it predictable that a civil war will break out at some point?

But what does civil war mean in a country where, per capita, every citizen owns at least one firearm, and in fact many own four, ten, twenty-five?

I don't think there will be a civil war like the Spanish Civil War, with armed multitudes clashing along a more or less defined front. No, this is not how the civil war of the postpolitical era of hypermedia dementia will unfold.

We will have a multiplication of racist shootings, we will have a multiplication of massacres, we will simply have what is already there, but increasingly widespread, harsh, violent.

In the 2020 investigative book *Deaths of Despair and the Future of Capitalism*, Anne Case and Angus Deaton describe the psycho-health situation of the demented giant: increased mortality, particularly among whites aged forty-five to fifty-four; alcoholism; suicide; use of firearms; obesity; and addiction to opioids (e.g., fentanyl). An overall drop in life expectancy (unique among advanced countries), from 78.8 years in 2014 to 76.3 years in 2021. All this in the presence of the highest health care costs in the world (equal to 18.8% of GDP).[9]

But this certainly does not mean that we can expect a peaceful disintegration of American power. Just as Polyphemus, blinded by Odysseus, slashes those who approach him, so the colossus is destined to react with reckless fury.

Since November 6, 2024, the overall winners of the latest round of American hell have begun to stage the spectacle of an orgy that announces the unleashing of racist violence on a scale that is hard to imagine.

The mass deportation of undocumented immigrants, on which Trump focused his electoral campaign, will hardly be able to be carried out legally. That Nazi-like project in itself can therefore only mean the return of the Ku Klux Klan to the cities and villages of the country.

Their industrial exploitation has never truly freed itself from the rules of slavery, which was formally imposed in its harshest form on millions of Black captives but continues today in the structural precariousness of work: total dependence, without any guarantees.

When slavery was abolished after the Civil War (the serious one, not the carnival and fragmentary one that kills without any reason other than madness), the Thirteenth Amendment to the US Constitution was approved. This amendment specified that slavery was no longer legal, with the exception of cases in which it was imposed as punishment for a crime.

From that moment on, the incarceration of African American people has been a constant fact in the history of the United States. In 2015, 55 percent of people incarcerated in America were Black, even though African Americans comprise only 12 percent of the total US population.

I don't know how it's going to end (nobody knows), but I make my prophecy, and I risk getting it right.

Media-demiurgic adventurism is already producing a disintegration of the global geopolitical reality, and will soon produce a disintegration of American society itself.

Those millions of American workers that Musk is gleefully threatening all have a shotgun in their basement. Tens of thousands of FBI officials, humiliated and treated like schoolchildren by a gang of merry rapists, manage databases and can throw the order of American life into a tailspin. The deep state really exists—it is not an invention of Steve Bannon—and sooner or later it is destined to take revenge to defend its filthy interests that Elon believes he can ignore. (And maybe Steve Bannon's militias will side with Musk's enemies.)

The Trumpists won the elections against a Democratic Party of corrupt hypocrites, but the hubris of the winners is giving rise to an underground nemesis that may soon explode, with the help of the wildfires in the cities and of the imminent future epidemics for which Kennedy has rolled out the red carpet.

Mutagenic Agents

Chaos and the automaton: these polarities define the process of mutation that is going to develop to completion, barring a terminal collapse of the human race that we are currently unable to foresee or rule out.

In recent times, catastrophic events have multiplied and chaos is expanding on planet Earth, while on the other hand decisive steps have been taken toward the total automation of human language and human life.

The political events of the last decade can certainly be defined as a reactionary turn, but beyond the political surface we may retrace double-edged evolutionary trends.

Take the emergence of Elon Musk as a worldwide kingmaker. Many commentators view the owner of Tesla as an agent of chaos. I think this characterization is too simplistic. Musk's goal only appears to be the promotion of chaos; in reality, his activity is aimed at the destruction of the state and of the social infrastructure. From this point of view, Musk's project mirrors that of Steve Bannon and the Trump Administration in general.

But Musk's multifaceted activity cannot be reduced to the final disintegration of the modern order (i.e., completion of the project begun by Thatcherite liberalism).

His activity is aimed at creating an infrastructure of total control of the communications system (Starlink), and at creating bio-digital interfaces that will enable the creation of fully intelligent automata (Neuralink).

After October 7, 2023, we have officially entered the age of global genocide: a proliferation of points of chaotic collapse. The global reactionary movement provokes chaotic breaking points everywhere.

But this is only one step of the process underway. The other step is the creation of a superior order, which is the order of the automaton.

The global reactionary movement today engages in the devastation of human society, which is the sphere of indeterminacy, approximation, analogy, and conjunction. But beyond the chaotic action of the reactionary movement, we can glimpse the emergence of a determinist, digital-connective order: the cognitive automaton that emerges from the wreckage of living chaos.

It can be said that Musk is an agent of political chaos, but the ultimate outcome will be the installation of an automated order.

In this process, life and language have to be reduced to functions of automatic self-generation: "functors," according to the definition proposed by the philosopher Rudolf Carnap.

A functor is an agent who is perfectly compliant and synchronized with the global cognitive automaton.

In order to enable compliance between human minds and artificial intelligence, two different operations are needed: alignment of the digital semio-machine to the human mind, and alignment of the human mind to the digital semio-machine.

During the first decades of the twenty-first century, the formatting of the human brain has been developed, and the synchronization of individual minds has been enabled.

In order to be compliant with the digital order, humans have been progressively deprived of characteristics and drives that are incompatible with the automaton, such as erotic desire, critical capacity, and generally expressive singularity.

This mutation cannot occur without enormous suffering, dysphoria, and depressive or aggressive psychopathologies.

For various reason (ideological resistance or psychological incompatibility), a part of the human race cannot be formatted and synchronized, and remains on the margins of the production process and the secured territory.

The nonformatted, nonsynchronized are going to be progressively eliminated through war, hunger, and other extermination techniques.

This is the horizon of the twenty-first century, clearly outlined by the political contours of Trumpism and by the techno-totalitarian activity of which Elon Musk is the linchpin.

A functionally superior and emotionally sterilized race of white males is taking over the levers of technical, economic, and military power. No political force can oppose this takeover, for the simple reason that it is not a political process but a techno-cognitive mutation. The endpoint of this process will be the replacement of human indeterminacy and fragility with organisms modified by genetic engineering—in other words, the elimination of the *Anthropos*, and the release of *Anthropos* 2.0.

Cognitive mutation and genocide are the two decisive processes of this passage.

Genocide is the massive elimination of those organisms that do not comply with the automaton. Cognitive mutation is achieved through the formatting of the human mind and its synchronization with the rhythm of the automaton.

Inevitably, this process of mutation involves suffering. Think of pathologies such as ADHD, or attention deficit hyperactivity disorder: this is not simply a pathology but an attempt to adapt and synchronize the mind to the hyperaccelerated rhythm of the info-sphere.

Ethical consciousness and erotic sensitivity are residuals of preformatted mankind that are rapidly disappearing in the emerging connective generation, the self-appointed last generation.

One of the main characteristics of this generation of mutants is the increasing inability to perceive the pain of others, which is in turn the ability to be functionally unempathetic. Some psychiatrists think that the rate of autistic spectrum disorder is increasing. Actually, I think that we should interpret this expansion of a so-called pathology as an adaptation to uninterrupted exposure to flows of painful nervous system stimuli.

The mutating mind is losing the ability to distinguish living organisms from electronic simulacra, and tends to consider suffering bodies as video game characters—little green men who do not suffer and can get back on their feet if they "die."

Climate collapse, geopolitical collapse, social collapse constitute the ideal environment for this process of mutation, formatting, and elimination of residual entities, although we should not dismiss the (very likely) possibility that the intertwining of these three collapses will produce the definitive extinction of the human race.

Everything that is human would be finally erased, and this would allow the perfect ideal of the Muskian Order to be realized: unlimited reproduction of the automaton in a territory purified of every chaotic and unpredictable element.

That said, deserters know that the unpredictable has not been cancelled and never will be.

5

THE AMERICAN UNCONSCIOUS AND THE DISINTEGRATION OF THE WESTERN WORLD

> Just as monstrous and mutant algae invade the lagoon of Venice, so our television screens are populated, saturated, by "degenerate" images and statements. In the field of social ecology, men like Donald Trump are permitted to proliferate freely, like another species of algae, taking over entire districts of New York and Atlantic City; he "redevelops" by raising rents, thereby driving out tens of thousands of poor families, most of whom are condemned to homelessness, becoming the equivalent of the dead fish of environmental ecology.
> —Félix Guattari, *The Three Ecologies*, 1989

> I am the last Cassandra of the human story. … I prophesied and nobody believed, and this time it's not only Troy that will burn, but Sparta and Ithaca and all the Achaeans too.
> —Salman Rushdie, *Quichotte*, 2020

The Trump Revolution in Two Moves

Do you remember what Joe Biden said a few months ago about the possibility of a Trump victory in the election?

More or less, he said that Trump's victory would destroy American democracy. He wasn't wrong: assuming that American democracy ever existed (which I don't believe), the advent of the Trump–Bannon–Musk gang represents its full-blown liquidation.

Technically speaking, the advent of Trump aims to be a revolution, albeit a reactionary one.

The Trumpist revolution will happen in two moves. The first move has been announced by Steve Bannon, the diabolical strategist, the most lucid of that merry band.

During Trump's first campaign, it was reported that once, at a party in 2013, Bannon had declared: "I'm a Leninist."[1]

The astonished writer to whom he said this asked for an explanation. Bannon replied: "Lenin wanted to destroy the state, and that's my goal too. I want to bring everything crashing down, and destroy all of today's establishment."[2]

But if for Lenin destroying the state was the prelude to building a proletarian dictatorship in the name of a future justice that never arrived, for Bannon destroying the state means allowing the profound dynamics of American society to be unleashed.

Here comes the second move, whose proponent would be Elon Musk: unleashing the animal spirits of American society, starting from a reactivation of the wild dynamics of this society, born from a genocide and enriched by dispossession and slavery.

Musk's project is the creation of a high-tech slave system, the abolition of residual social protections, the systematic use of terror against minorities and immigrants. The implementation of this programmatic framework can be glimpsed in the declarations and in the first steps of the DOGE project.

Pretending that the United States is a democracy (as if that word means anything) implies a state of systematic denial, a stubborn repression (in the Freudian sense of *Verdrängung*) of the psychogenesis of the American unconscious.

Before dying, just a few months ago, Paul Auster wrote a book, *Bloodbath Nation*, that tries to come to terms with the reality (and the unconscious) of the American entity.

Auster remarks that in Berlin, there is a monument dedicated to the memory of the Holocaust. In Washington, there is nothing dedicated to centuries of slavery.[3]

Racism is the core of the American unconscious. This is why Trump is the soul of America.

Better said: Trump is the psychotic eruption of the senescent white unconscious, unable to deal with the amount of violence that haunts the country's collective self-perception, and unable to deal with its decline (demographically, mentally, politically).

Trump is the violent expulsion of the unbearable self-loathing of white culture.

The Empire, from Augustus to Caligula

Twenty-five years ago, two eminent philosophers wrote in a book that received widespread attention:

> Empire is … the sovereign power that governs the world. … Empire is emerging today as the center that supports the globalization of productive networks and casts its widely inclusive net to try to envelop all power relations within its world order. … We should understand the society of control … as that society … in which mechanisms of command become ever more "democratic," ever more immanent to the social field, distributed throughout the brains and bodies of the citizens.[4]

Dazzled by the light of the Clinton era, Michael Hardt and Antonio Negri were missing the nihilistic substance of US global hegemony, and the destructive nature of the new technologies dependent on the neoliberal model. Their book proposed to view postmodern empire as equivalent to the progressive trend implicit in the utopia of networked revolution.

"This imperial project, a global project of network power, defines the fourth phase or regime of U.S. constitutional history," they wrote.[5]

Hardt and Negri were expecting peace and prosperity based on the peer-to-peer principle, because they failed to see the duplicity of that principle, and also because they did not grasp the irredeemable abyss of the American unconscious.

Also in the year 2000, Salman Rushdie published a highly prophetic book, *Fury*. Let's read some lines:

> [New York was] this Metropolis built of Kryptonite in which no Superman dared set foot, where wealth was mistaken for riches and the joy of possession for happiness, where people lived such polished lives that the great rough truths of raw existence had been rubbed and buffed away, and in which human souls had wandered so separately for so long that they barely remembered how to touch; this city whose fabled electricity powered the electric fences that were being erected between men and men, and men and women, too.[6]

The tension that ran beneath the surface of globalism at the beginning of the century was not perceived by the authors of *Empire*, who instead wrote:

> Empire can only be conceived as a universal republic, a network of powers and counterpowers structured in a boundless and inclusive architecture. This imperial expansion has nothing to do with imperialism, nor with those state organisms designed for conquest, pillage, genocide, colonization, and slavery. Against such imperialisms, Empire extends and consolidates the model of network power.[7]

A few months after the publication of *Empire*, the new economy based on digital technology collapsed worldwide. Eventually, in the year 2001, al-Qaeda set in motion the war that unfolded in the terrorist wave of Daesh and in the counterterrorist wars in Iraq, Afghanistan, and so on.

This evolution totally escapes the theoretical schema outlined in *Empire*: "An idea of peace is at the basis of the development and expansion of Empire. This is an immanent idea of peace that is dramatically opposed to the transcendent idea of peace, that is, the peace that only the transcendent sovereign can impose on a society whose nature is defined by war. Here, on the contrary, nature is peace."[8] On the same page, Hardt and Negri quote Virgil: "The final age that the oracle foretold has arrived; / The great order of the centuries is born again."[9]

Shortly after the publication of this book, the history of the world took a totally different direction. The *coup de théâtre* of 9/11 reversed the prevailing sense of the invincibility of Western hegemony.

The never-ending peaceful expansion of democracy gave way to the breakdown of the global hegemony of the United States.

After a decade of inconclusive wars, of social decline, and of growing resentment, the emergence of Donald Trump marked the beginning of a sort of chaotic civil war in the very center of the empire.

Now, twenty-five years later, the civil war in the United States is provisionally over, and it's easy to understand who the (provisional) winner is. The winner is not Augustus, the glorious and peace-loving emperor glorified by Virgil, but an interesting mix of Caligula and Nero.

The problem of Hardt and Negri, the reason why their book failed to grasp the impending process, lies in their indifference to the anthropological dimension of American politics.

Only by gauging the abyss of the American unconscious can we decipher the roots of the social ferocity that is now on full display.

Unthinkable

Much more interesting than Hardt and Negri's book is Jamie Raskin's *Unthinkable: Trauma, Truth, and the Trials of American Democracy.*

Published in 2022, on the first anniversary of the farcical insurrection that brought thousands of Trump's followers into the political heart of the United States, the book takes on a new meaning today, after the comeback of the leader of that subversive demonstration.

The author is a Democratic congressman from Maryland. Jamie Raskin is also a professor of constitutional law, a self-proclaimed liberal, and a father of three. One of his children, Tommy, twenty-five years old—a political activist, a supporter of progressive causes, a compassionate, empathetic young man—died on the last day of 2020.

To be more precise, Tommy committed suicide, because of a long-lasting depression, and also (it goes without saying) because of the long moral humiliation of his humanitarian values during the years of the first Trump presidency.

This book has been important for me, because it contains a radical reflection on the entrenched racism of American democracy (a detail that totally escaped the self-appointed Marxists who wrote *Empire*).

For Jamie Raskin, Tommy's death was not only an emotional trauma but also a call to a radical meditation on the depth of the crisis that is tearing apart liberal democracy.

I read the book just after its publication and I'm reading it again now that Trump's comeback buries forever the credibility of American democracy, and questions the very credibility of the concept of democracy itself.

Raskin writes that he has always considered himself as "an optimist … radically optimistic about how the Constitution of the nation itself can uplift our social, political, and intellectual condition."[10]

After the death of his son, however, his self-perception has changed. He writes that his constitutional optimism has been shattered by the predominance of brutal force over the force of reason, and by the spread of depression.

> Suddenly, this constitutional optimism shames and embarrasses me. … I fear that my sunny political optimism, what many of my friends have treasured in me most, has become a trap for massive self-delusion, a weakness to be exploited by our enemies.

> Yet I am also terrified to think about what it would mean to live without this buoyancy—and also without my beloved, irreplaceable son. The two always went hand-in-hand, and now I may be alive on earth without either of them.[11]

The political optimism of this generous law professor has been shaken by the sudden realization that liberal democracy rests on a fragile foundation. Indeed, he writes: "Four out of our first five presidents were slave masters from Virginia, and seven of our first ten presidents were slaveholders. These facts were not contingent or random but arose from the deep architecture of our political institutions."[12]

Slavery is part of the American nation's cultural heritage, like the genocide of the early inhabitants of its territory.

How can this nation claim to be seen as an example to others?

How can we avoid thinking that this nation is a danger to the survival of humanity?

It's now becoming impossible to persist in a state of denial: the American memory is so loaded with horror that no political evolution can erase this elementary truth from the collective unconscious of a country whose manifest destiny is the destruction of the whole of humanity.

In the speech that Biden gave on January 6, 2022, one year after the bizarre insurrection, speaking of the need to reject violence, he said: "We must decide: What kind of nation are we going to be?"[13]

Can America decide to rule out violence, if American history is based on the violence of slavery and genocide?

The irreparability of that past is a source of chronic depression for the West, and therefore a source of chronic violence. But now, if we look at the geopolitical landscape, if we look at the inner landscape of Western culture, disintegration seems irreversible.

Will the decline and disintegration of the Western world trigger the final destruction of what we used to call civilization?

Disintegration

In my humble opinion, Trump's election will accelerate Western disintegration. The mass deportation that has been has promised by the winners will result in a restaging of the Ku Klux Klan in many areas of the country rather than in an actual—impossible—operation of deporting undocumented immigrants. Violence, fear, aggressiveness will eventually persuade immigrants to go away, in a process that will hardly be peaceful.

Despair will be the driving force of American disintegration.

In an article published on *e-flux* after Trump's victory, Slavoj Žižek relativizes the Trumpian triumph, and tries to put it in perspective. The MAGA formula can be described in an inverted way: after decades of military defeats, the superpower recognizes that it cannot continue the policy of global hegemony and must withdraw by accepting, without admitting it, a position of local power that must compete on an equal footing with other local powers—Russia, China, India.

Žižek's opinion is well founded, but my question is, Will the stronghold of white supremacy accept its decline without a reaction that might be nothing short of apocalyptic?

Furthermore, Žižek thinks that Europe could emerge stronger from the downsizing of America's geopolitical role, a possibility hidden behind the promise of making America great again. Europe, according to Žižek, will no longer be the "little sister" of the giant.[14]

Here too I have some doubts. Žižek's hypothesis would be true only if the EU really existed. But the Ukrainian war has pushed the European Union into a position of irrelevance, weakness, and rapid disintegration.

The French government is breaking down, the German government is breaking down, while economic recession is looming.

The strategic defeat in the war against Putin's Russia (the legacy of Biden) pushes the EU toward disintegration, while the allies of Putin, election after election, are winning the majority of the continent's parliamentary seats.

To conclude my short essay, I will quote Salman Rushdie again: "I can't look up. Up there, what is that. Like a colossus with a huge blaster blew a hole in the air. You look at it, you want to die. This can't be fixed. I don't believe there's anyone in DC or Canaveral who knows what the fuck to do about *this*."[15]

6

HYPERCOLONIALISM AND SEMIO-CAPITAL

> CALIBAN. You taught me language, and my profit on't
> Is, I know how to curse. The red plague rid you
> For learning me your language!
> —Shakespeare, *The Tempest*

During the years 2024 and 2025, Europe descends into open war with Russia, and the elections in France and Germany only accelerate the disintegration of the European Union.

Everywhere, liberal democracy marches toward war. Everywhere, nationalism festers.

Meanwhile, Israel, a nuclear superpower, continues its suicidal spiral, killing all those who dare to exist in its sightline—chiefly the Palestinians, but now Lebanon and Syria as well. Notwithstanding Israel's military superiority in Gaza and beyond (due in large part to US support), internal divisions and international isolation, which are already evident, will only feed a psychotic crisis as the horror of genocide continues.

For decades, Netanyahu has been deluding himself and the Israeli people that Hamas could be a useful tool for dividing the Palestinians in Gaza and the West Bank.[11]

Even before October 7, many Israeli commentators, such as Gideon Levy, wondered whether Israel's legitimacy and future were faltering.[2]

While Palestinians fight against dehumanization and occupation, and while Ukraine defends against an invasion, there is another war playing out in the center of empire that we cannot ignore.

It is being waged by different segments of the white, European, elite power structure: between neoliberal imperialism and the rising Trumputinism, a mix of white supremacism and nationalist aggressiveness. Trumputinism is the final offensive against the oppressed of the earth, when the Global South is in turmoil and a million migrants are on the move in any corner of the planet.

This is why Gaza has become the symbol of the tremendous epoch in which we live: because Israeli genocide is the symbol of contemporary hypercolonialist violence.

Perhaps, emerging from this war amongst empire's elites, one can find new orienting concepts and novel maps for desertion. To do so, we must first attend to how colonialism is different today from in the past.

Reassessing Colonialism

For many, Gaza has been and continues to be the symbol of the return of colonialism, which many had erroneously assigned to the dustbin of the twentieth century. Prefixes such as *post-* aside, resistance movements across the world have shown for many decades that colonial projects never ended, they just changed character.

The history of colonialism is a history of land predation. Historically, it targeted resource-rich places to fulfill the needs of Western accumulation. Millions of men and women were exploited and subjected to colonial rule, or expelled to the territories of the colonizing power. It is impossible to describe the formation of the industrial-capitalist system in Europe without considering that this process was preceded and accompanied by the violent subjugation of non-European territories and the enslavement of millions of people.

Many have underlined this logic, which Cedric Robinson has called "racial capitalism."[3] In his book *Black Marxism*, he demonstrates the key role of racist oppression and slavery in the accumulation of capital on the European continent and in the New World. Furthermore, as many scholars of anticolonialism have noted, perhaps most famously Aimé Césaire, European fascism was in some respects the application of the practices of colonial governance to the metropole—in the case of Nazism, targeting Jewish, communist, queer, and Romani populations.[4]

This fact is so clear that even someone such as Zbigniew Brzezinski, who served as national security advisor to Jimmy Carter, had to admit in 2016:

> Periodic massacres of their not-so-distant ancestors by colonists and associated wealth-seekers largely from western Europe (countries that today are, still tentatively at least, most open to multiethnic cohabitation) resulted within the past two or so centuries in the slaughter of colonized peoples on a scale comparable to Nazi World War II crimes: literally involving hundreds of thousands and even millions of victims. … Just as shocking as the scale of these atrocities is how quickly the West forgot about them.[5]

Indeed, historical memory is very selective, especially when it comes to the crimes of European civilization. In particular, the memory of the extermination of non-European peoples is not given special attention and is not part of mainstream collective memory, unlike the Shoah.[6]

The British, Belgians, French, Italians, and others also exterminated entire populations as part of a larger project to impose European economic and political domination. Yet they are not as frequently invoked outside circles on the Left or in academia; for those who control mainstream attention, it would appear that Hitler alone deserves to be forever execrated—perhaps because the majority of his victims did not have Black skin. A caricature of those who carried out the genocide of Indigenous peoples of North America is even celebrated in a heroic cult designed by Hollywood.

It is well known that colonialism unleashed irreversible material effects on the globe—for example, what

Andreas Malm refers to as "fossil capitalism"; however, colonialism also tremendously affected the social and psychological spheres, as attended to most powerfully, perhaps, by Frantz Fanon.[7] The anticolonialist movements of the twentieth century ultimately failed to transform political sovereignty into economic, cultural, and military autonomy—in large part because of neocolonial, counterinsurgent interventions by colonial powers.[8]

Today, colonialism continues apace, albeit with new, what we might call "deterritorialized," techniques and modalities, regardless of the formal sovereignty enjoyed (so to speak) by countries in the Global South.

Hypercolonialism: The Extraction of Cognitive Resources

Since the "deterritorialization" of global capitalism—in other words, its globalization and financialization—the relationship between the Global North and South has entered a phase of "hypercolonization." I use the term to refer more precisely to these new modalities of colonial aggression and governance. Their appearance does not signal the end of "old" techniques—whether extractivism or open theft—but rather indicates the rise of new forms of digital extraction from workers who physically remain in the Global South but produce value in a deterritorialized, fragmented, and technologically coordinated manner.

Today, the extraction of value from the Global South takes place partly in the semiotic sphere: the digital capture of very cheap labor, essentially digital slavery, in sectors such as logistics and even agriculture. These are some of the modes of hypercolonial exploitation integrated into the circuits of what I have been for many years calling "semio-capitalism."

While some continue to erroneously think of slavery as a precapitalist phenomenon because of its decisive role in the so-called primitive accumulation of capital, it is now abundantly clear that slavery continues in an extended and pervasive form thanks to digital modalities of governance and deterritorialized coordination.

The global assembly line has been restructured in a geographically dislocated form: the workers who run the global network live in places thousands of miles apart, and it is partially because of this fragmentation that they are unable to set in motion a process of organization and autonomy.

The formation of digital platforms has created productive subjects who did not exist before the 1980s: a digital labor force that cannot be recognized as a social subject due to the precariousness and fragmentation of its internal composition. Platform capitalism creates two tiers of subjugation and employment. A small minority of the workforce is involved in the design and marketing of so-called immaterial products, earning high wages and identifying with the company and its nominally liberal values. Simultaneously, a much more numerous and geographically dispersed workforce performs maintenance, tagging, and other cleanup tasks for online platforms for very low wages, and has no unions or political representation. Often, these workers are hired by subcontractors and almost completely disconnected from the companies exploiting their labor power. In extreme cases, they might not even think of themselves as workers since their meager wages are paid in progressively more invisible forms. This new digital workforce took shape between the 1990s and the first decade of the new century, under conditions that make autonomy and solidarity almost impossible. Perhaps the signal example of this workforce is the workers of Amazon's Mechanical Turk "crowdsourcing marketplace," documented in Hans Block and Moritz Riesewieck's 2019 film *The Cleaners*, which chronicles conditions of acute material and psychological exploitation.

There have been isolated attempts by digital workers to organize unions or to challenge their companies. I am thinking, for example, of the eight thousand Google workers who stood up against their employer's subordination to the US military-industrial complex.[9] This and similar manifestations of solidarity have occurred where the digital workforce is assembled in large numbers and earns high wages.

In his book *The Drowned and the Saved*, the Italian-Jewish author Primo Levi writes that when he was interned in a concentration camp, he hoped for solidarity among fellow prisoners but had to recognize that they were "a thousand sealed off monads, and between them a desperate covert and continuous struggle."[10]

He describes this space as "the gray zone" because the binary of victim/perpetrator was inapplicable, since law and morality were absent.[11] Under conditions of extreme violence and permanent terror, those involved were forced to constantly think about their own survival and they failed to create bonds of solidarity with other exploited people. As in the death camps, as in the cotton plantations of the slave states in the Southern US, the immaterial and material slave circuit that digital globalization has helped to create seems to thwart the conditions for solidarity.

This is what I want to point to with the word *hypercolonialism*. It is a dependent function of semio-capitalism: the violent extraction of mental resources and attention under conditions of deterritorialization.

Hypercolonialism and Migration: The Expanding Genocide

But hypercolonialism is not just evident in the extraction of cognitive labor. It is perhaps most visible in the exceedingly violent control of the flows of immigration—whether in the Mediterranean or along the US–Mexico border. This is also intimately related to the changes to the global, racialized capitalist mode of production brought about by semio-capitalism, which has altered the conditions for the global circulation of information and wealth.

The increasingly infertile, senescent, economically declining, and culturally depressed people of the Global North see the migrant masses as a danger. They fear that the poor of the earth will bring their misery to the wealthy metropolises. Migrants are portrayed as the cause of the misfortunes suffered by the privileged minority. A class of politicians who specialize in sowing racial hatred delude old white men into believing that if someone could wipe out that disturbing mass of young people pressing at the gates of the fortress, if someone could destroy them, annihilate them, then the good times would return. America would be great again, and the moribund white homeland would regain its youth.

In the past decade, the line that divides the North from the South, which runs from the Mexico–Texas border to the Mediterranean Sea to the forests of Central and Eastern Europe, has become the battleground of a nefarious war—the black heart of global genocide. This is a genocidal war against unarmed people, exhausted by hunger and fatigue, assaulted by armed policemen, dogs, sadistic fascists, and above all by the forces of nature supercharged by climate change: the rivers, the seas, the desert.

Despite the glowing commodity advertisements that stimulate consumerist idiots, despite neoliberal propaganda, the logic of semio-capital continues. Because the Global North infiltrates the South through the innumerable tentacles of the web, populations press for access to territories where the climate is still tolerable, where there is water, where war has not yet arrived with all its destructive force. But these populations are repelled by armed police and genocide.

In the Global North, a significant part (if not the majority) of the white population has decided to barricade itself inside the fortress and use any means to repel the migrant wave—whether parliamentary or extrajudicial. Yesterday's colonialists, who crossed the seas to invade foreign lands, now cry "invasion" at the sight of millions pressing against the fortress gates.

Marxism's Omissions

In the early work of Marx and Engels, the role of colonialism is scantly addressed, apart from a few passages. In *The Communist Manifesto*, for example, Western imperialism is essentially glossed as a progressive force that brings underdeveloped societies to a level of bourgeois civilization, paving the way for the formation of a global proletariat. In *Capital*, however, Marx demonstrates a keen, if not fully developed, awareness of the relationship between colonialism, the slave trade, and the origins of industrial capitalism. The part on "primitive accumulation," in the first volume, is devoted to analyzing those processes. Colonial subjugation, the slave trade, and the exploitation of child labor are discussed here, albeit briefly. (Throughout *Capital*, Marx also devotes attention to Ireland.) As the famous first paragraph of this part reads:

> We have seen how money is transformed into capital; how surplus-value is made through capital, and how more capital is made from surplus-value. But the accumulation of capital presupposes surplus-value; surplus-value presupposes capitalist production;

> capitalist production presupposes the availability of considerable masses of capital and of labour-power in the hands of commodity producers. The whole movement, therefore, seems to turn around in a never-ending circle, which we can only get out of by assuming a primitive accumulation (the "previous accumulation" of Adam Smith) which precedes capitalist accumulation; an accumulation which is not the result of the capitalist mode of production but its point of departure.[12]

In the chapter titled "The Genesis of the Industrial Capitalist," Marx examines the colonization of India: "Between 1769 and 1770, the English created a famine by buying up all the rice and refusing to sell it again, except at fabulous prices."[13] And: "While the cotton industry introduced child-slavery into England, in the United States it gave the impulse for the transformation of the earlier, more or less patriarchal slavery into a system of commercial exploitation. In fact the veiled slavery of the wage-labourers in Europe needed the unqualified slavery of the New World as its pedestal."[14]

Aside from a few exceptions, in much orthodox Marxist theory the question of colonialism remained poorly understood from a strategic perspective. A certain degree of Eurocentrism is constitutive of this Marxist point of view. Even in Lenin's writings, including *Imperialism, the Highest Stage of Capitalism*, the question is not fully developed. One had to wait until the 1960s for the topic of colonialism to come to the forefront of internationalist labor movements. Still, a strategic perspective was not fully defined except in signal works such as Walter Rodney's *How Europe Underdeveloped Africa*, published in 1972.

During those years, the anticolonial movement transformed global power relations. Even after gaining national sovereignty, however, colonized peoples across the world were unable to emancipate themselves from the economic subservience that five centuries of systematic exploitation and devastation had forced upon them. Perhaps only Maoism brought the colonial question to the center of revolutionary strategy. But can we really regard Mao Zedong as a Marxist thinker? Or should we rather regard him as the forerunner of a non-Eurocentric vision that went beyond the limits of Marxist theory?

All these questions about the relationship between global capitalism and imperialism have returned today with brutal urgency, but the ability to think in internationalist terms seems to have waned. Today, collective thought recoils in horror at the idea of nuclear war becoming possible again, of genocide's endlessness. After the liquidation of workers' internationalism, only capital has remained capable of offering a global vision—one comprised not of concepts but of financial algorithms and abstractions.

Despite the formal decolonization of the 1950s and '60s, despite all the talk of postcolonialism in academia, colonized peoples are more oppressed today than ever before. But the general form of colonialism has changed profoundly, in parallel with the changing processes of capitalist valorization. Indeed, some of the language and ideals of past revolts against colonial forces have been adopted by movements with a nationalist character—for example, the right-wing ethno-nationalist Hindutva movement led by Narendra Modi—and have triggered an explosion of chaotic conflicts.

It is urgently necessary to consider the new modalities and forms of colonialism in the twenty-first century. Only then can we understand how these chaotic conflicts are unfolding. Only then can we imagine how our defection might unfold.

7

MARX AND DARWIN

According to Marx, the solution to the historical enigma called alienation can be found in the relation between technology and labor—better said, in the relation between the refusal of labor and the evolution of technology.

Communism is the conscious evolution of this relation, based on the force of social autonomy of the organized workers.

According to an apocryphal anecdote, Marx intended to dedicate *Capital* to Charles Darwin, and Darwin politely declined the proposal. In a letter signed and dated October 13, 1880, Darwin wrote: "I Shd. prefer the Part or Volume not be dedicated to me (though I thank you for the intended honor)."[1]

It is now known that this exchange between Marx and Darwin did not really occur, but the story is curious, and invites me to reflect on the relationship between Marx's thought and Darwin's thought.[2]

There is no doubt that Marx and Engels had a very high opinion of the work of the English naturalist.

Engels, who intended to study natural science in depth from a dialectical perspective, read *On the Origin of Species* as soon as the book arrived in bookstores in 1859, and wrote to Marx: "Darwin, by the way, whom I'm reading just now, is absolutely splendid. There was one aspect of teleology that had yet to be demolished, and that has now been done. Never before has so grandiose an attempt been made to demonstrate historical evolution in Nature, and certainly never to such good effect."[3]

The Darwinian vision therefore allows us to free the natural sciences from teleology, just as Marx and Engels were freeing human history from teleology.

In the introduction to the *Grundrisse* (known as the introduction of '57), Marx writes: "Human anatomy contains a key to the anatomy of the ape. The intimations of higher development among the subordinate animal species, however, can be understood only after the higher development is already known. The bourgeois economy thus supplies the key to the ancient."[4]

In the essay "Marx in the Sieve of Darwin," Dominique Lecourt argues that in Darwin's book, Marx found a "historico-natural foundation" for his own conception.[5]

And in a letter to Lassalle, Marx writes again: "Darwin's work is most important … in that it provides a basis in natural science for the historical class struggle."[6]

We are used to reading Marx as someone who extended, albeit in a critical and innovative way, the historical dialectic that has its foundation in Hegelian idealism. As much as Marx distanced himself from Hegel—to the point of stating that he wanted to overthrow him to put dialectics back on its feet, which in Hegel appeared "standing on its head"—we have continued to consider him a dialectical thinker.[7]

Marx goes beyond the Hegelian dialectical methodology, and in his maturity the teleological tension implicit in the concept of history is replaced by the materialistic dynamics of social forces that oppose capitalist domination and emerge as autonomous subjectivities.

Even if Marx soon emancipated himself from the idea that history is the process of realization of the Spirit, he still remained convinced (so it seems, at least) that history was the realization of something.

What exactly, we don't know.

Communism? In fact, for Marx, communism is not an ideal to be achieved, nor even a program, but the abolition of the present state of things: the abolition of private property, of exploitation, of the accumulation of abstract value.

At this point, any finality is abandoned.

What interests us is the dynamics. The end is nothing, the movement is everything.

For this reason, we can say that Marx's thought falls within the sphere of Darwinian thought understood as the thought of evolution that takes place according to the rules of natural selection and that has no finality, no teleological or transcendent meaning.

In evolution, there is no plan, there is no intention, just an imbalance between forces, conflict, and the adaptation of the organism to a changing and dangerous environment. What we call history is the illusion that this natural selection is the pursuit of ideals or projects. Thanks to this illusion, we believe in free will, we believe in politics.

But the idea of free will is just an idealistic superstition that covers with fake heroism the brutal selection that allows collective entities (populations, nations, social classes) to conquer a vital space at the expense of other collective entities.

As in nature, so in human affairs (in that process that, bombastically, we call history): the forces (the jumble of forces) that are best suited to integration with the environment (physical, psychological, etc.) prevail.

In this sense, Marx's thought is similar to Darwin's thought, but this conceptual analogy must be handled with great care.

In the last decades of the twentieth century, a philosophy called social Darwinism prevailed in liberal ideology, which exalts the market as the place in which fitness, or adaptation to the environment, is defined by competitiveness—that is, by the ability to respond to social needs.

According to this ideology, the particularism of the strongest and most suitable is destined to defeat and subjugate all other particularisms.

Natural selection then re-presented itself in neoliberal ideology as the predominance of the most competitive, and as the elimination of those who are not capable of keeping up with the pace of the competitive economy.

This logic has extended from the economy to every sphere of social and geopolitical relations, with the result of transforming the world—as has actually happened since the 1980s—into a jungle where everywhere there is a struggle for survival and the majority of social actors succumb or live miserably, because the fittest (those who've constructed the environment according to their private interests) survive and prosper at the expense of all others, and at the expense of the environment itself, which has been transformed into an unlivable hell for the vast majority of humans.

This new version of liberalism is more ferocious than that of Adam Smith, because while the founder of classical liberalism recognized the need to respect the rights of society, Margaret Thatcher stated that society does not exist: only individuals, families, and companies exist, and their only agenda is the pursuit of maximum profit.

From that moment on, capitalism became absolutism of profit: no law, no rule that opposes the full, free expansion of the exploitation of human and natural resources has more value. Deregulation is the unleashing of the animal spirits of business.

Neoliberals have rightly claimed to be Darwinians who extend the principle of natural selection to the sphere of social relations.

How can we therefore affirm that Marx's thought fits into the context of evolutionism? How can we believe that Marx accepts the principle of natural selection—that is, the principle according to which in human history, as in the natural world, whoever prevails is always the most suitable for the environment (i.e., the strongest)?

Don't we thus run the risk of abandoning all universalism and every prospect of emancipation from exploitation, and above all of betraying the egalitarianism that constitutes the fundamental principle of the workers' movement inspired by Marxism?

Here we find the *coup de génie* of Marxist materialism, which I would like to illustrate.

Communist egalitarianism is not an ideal principle that political will can implement in the history of class struggles.

Marx does not propose the realization of the egalitarian ideal: egalitarianism is not a principle, nor an objective, but the process that, from the abstraction of work and practical equality between workers, moves toward the creation of a society in which economic equality is the condition of the freedom of cultural differences.

Marx does not believe in political democracy, he does not believe in law. He does not believe that political dialectics can overturn relations between classes. Only social struggle can do this. He knows very well that the law is the formalization of a relationship of force, he knows very well that political democracy is a very fragile framework in which ultimately, despite legal and formal equality, relationships between classes are imposed.

The real game is played in the balance of power between social classes.

History proceeds through a sort of natural selection in which the strongest, the most suited to the social environment, imposes its interests and its rules.

In this sense, we can say that Marx's thought falls within the sphere of evolutionism.

But for Marx, industrial capitalism has created a class that suffers from radical alienation: the working class, an increasingly vast mass of people to whom capital offers the possibility of survival (i.e., of reproducing itself as a mere workforce), but from whom it takes away everything that can be defined as human.

It takes away the freedom to live one's own time, it takes away the pleasures of existence, it takes away dignity and breath. To define this radical expropriation, Marx borrows the (ambiguous) Hegelian word "alienation."

The subject of historical knowledge is the oppressed class that struggles for emancipation. This class is seen by Marx as the universal avenger, the social subject that completes the work of liberation for the sake of generations of defeated people.

The working class cannot emancipate itself from its particular condition without questioning all forms of oppression, exploitation, and impoverishment of collective existence. The emancipation of this class cannot occur unless the entire human race is emancipated from capitalism, from the law of value and also from war, from the violence that arises from the particularism of capital.

The particularism of the working class is the bearer of universality.

Therefore Marx does not betray the universalist intention that finds its most complete form in social equality and political internationalism.

Internationalism is not an abstract principle of universal brotherhood; it is not a Kantian moral imperative but the political expression of workers' interests, which has nothing to do with the nation.

French workers and German workers have the same interests, they have no reason to fight against each other.

As long as capital holds the power to force men to submit to its interests, French and German workers will be forced to wear the national uniform, pick up a rifle, and go to muddy places to be killed in order to defend a frontier that means nothing to them.

In this sense, Marx does not betray the universalist vocation that Jewish culture had brought about into modernity.

On the contrary, he brings this vocation to its completion: not only universalism of rights but also concrete universality of social justice.

Marxist universalism, unlike that of the Enlightenment, is not based on reason but on force. In this, Marx can be considered Darwinian.

But the force to which Marx refers cannot pursue its particular interest (freeing itself from capitalist exploitation) without pursuing the interest of the entire society. In this sense, the working class is, so to speak, a universalizing force.

Through class struggle, working-class strength makes democracy possible as an affirmation of the interests of the entire society.

We know well that the working class does not exist: there are individual workers, those who own nothing, who have been expropriated from their land by the enclosures, and consequently are forced to sell their lives and their time to earn a salary with which to buy bread to feed their children, a workforce that will in turn be exploited in the future.

And for this reason, someone called them "proletarians."

These individuals are forced to work together in horrible places called factories and to carry out tiring and degrading tasks to increase the master's capital, and at a certain point they become a class because they are united by the practical conviction of being a class.

Internationalist communism is the mythology that allows these separate individuals to become part of a unitary and powerful social body.

Only when the working class—this imaginary entity that exists because millions of people are aware (or delude themselves, if you prefer) of being part of it—exercises its hegemony over the whole of society can particular interest become universal interest.

In these conditions, natural selection can veer toward egalitarianism, solidarity, the collective pleasure of collaboration.

Marx's thought thus managed to free Darwinian selection from its brutality, while the social Darwinism that is at the heart of neoliberalism (or capitalist absolutism) sees no possibility of emancipating itself from particularism and cannot conceive of force except as the oppression of someone by someone else.

Democracy acts as a common good only when the working class (the universal class) possesses sufficient strength to impose itself on the (particular) domination of profit.

Internationalism would be a utopia if it were not the expression of millions of people who, despite living in many different places, do not belong to any fucking nation, and their way of living and thinking were not reducible to traditions nor to the characteristics of a national identity or an ethnicity.

These millions of men and women are the working class, as long as it exists (existed) as a shared illusion.

If that shared illusion dissolves—as I fear has happened in the neoliberal era, for material, structural, and psychological reasons—then all that remains is what we have around us now: idiotic particularism, the rhetoric of the nation and of war.

Here, then, comes Darwin's grim face, which Marx had sought to soften: without internationalism, the law of the strongest returns, or of the most fit to survive, which means the most armed, the most ruthless, the most brutal.

Ferocity returns.

And pity disappears, which is not a religious feeling but the ability to recognize in others the sensitive continuation of the self.

History/Evolution

In the modern era, we have conceived of history as the effect of the conscious activity of humans aimed at emancipating social life from the pitiless laws of evolution, as evolution is a process by which some organisms proliferate to the detriment of less suited organisms.

I do not use the word "pitiless" by chance.

Pietas is the essential difference between life subject to the laws of evolution and life progressing in the conscious sphere of history.

Pietas is not just a moral feeling but it is solidarity between those who face the harshness of nature together, and experiment together with the possibilities of common intelligent action. *Pietas* is a condition of cooperation between groups and individuals, regardless of their place on the evolutionary hierarchy.

Pietas can be translated as "solidarity."

The rhetoric of civilization can ultimately be reduced to this: the history of human collectives differs from nature in that it emancipates itself from implacable natural selection, introducing universal principles of justice in the relationships between groups and individuals. As we have seen, Marx does not believe much in these principles, or at least he does not believe in the possibility of making universal principles operational in real history, because the vital interests of individuals and classes prevail over principles—bending them, distorting them, or canceling them—if they have the strength to do so.

In Marx, human evolution becomes history when social classes develop projects and consciously organize themselves to carry them out.

Politics would be the technique that allows the will to pursue and impose its projects, so as to escape from the blindly evolutionary dimension and enter the dimension of historical consciousness.

The Enlightenment and the culture of democracy have proposed a legal regulation of collective behavior. But legal regulation works as long as the concrete actors of the game recognize the ethical validity of the rules, as long as the rules do not conflict with the material interests of those actors.

Marx proposes to found politics on a more Darwinian basis, if I may say so: politics is the organization of interests in the form of projects, and the working class has actually been able to put into practice a politics in which particular interest coincides with the interest of the great majority of society, an egalitarian politics based on a partisan material interest.

In our times, however, this possibility seems to have disappeared since workers, due to neoliberal deregulation and digitalization, find themselves in conditions of isolation, since they find themselves in continuous competition, due to precariousness.

Evolution has regained its place in history since free will has proved inefficient, and consequently the political processes have lost their material potency.

Now we find ourselves in this ultimate condition in which the potency of technical automatisms has become ungovernable, and the trends that we can peruse on the horizon of the twenty-first century surpass the potencies of will and politics.

Earlier in the modern era, some large processes—not all, of course—were governable by the voluntary action of associated humans. In the complexity of planetary and social evolution, politics had managed to carve out areas in which the will was powerful: it was able to govern the construction of industrial infrastructure, to impose state sovereignty on social dynamics and national territories. Will was also able to enforce a regulation of some economic flows …

This sphere in which the will of individuals, groups, and nations could determine decisive processes was called history. In that context, it was possible to shape evolution by removing it from the determinisms of nature.

There were domains in which political decisions could do nothing, or could do very little: epidemics, demography, unpredictable meteorological events remained ungovernable, relegated to the background of history.

Additionally, the social imagination remained largely ungoverned by political will.

The human agent took pride in the successes of the will, and attributed to themselves a power greater than that which they actually enjoyed.

Humans grew persuaded that will could dominate the complexity of reality, but this was an illusion.

Today that illusion has fallen: organized and voluntary action is no longer able to govern more than a tiny, perhaps irrelevant, part of the great processes that engulf the existence of the planet's population. Let's think about climate change, the effects of which have repercussions on migration, on the collective unconscious, and on the imagination, giving rise to an unstoppable movement of a furiously reactionary nature.

Spreading psychosis, mass depression among younger generations, depressing effects of senility, and last but not least, the expanding refusal of procreation are trends that politics is unable to control or govern.

Demography is a domain in which political will has almost no control: the demographic explosion in the past century was neither planned nor plannable, even if progress in the fields of medicine and nutrition favored that explosion. And in the twenty-first century, the reduction of the birth rate is a trend that cannot be changed by the forces of will and law, even if its biopolitical and psycho-political consequences may be catastrophic.

On the climate, on demography, on psychopathology we can do nothing, or very little. For this reason, those who deny the existence of the climate crisis win elections. They deny our impotence and dedicate their efforts to railing against and threatening imaginary enemies, sublimating impotence into the desire for revenge against a phantom enemy such as immigrants.

When the will is emptied of all power, the historical event is reduced to its biopolitical and psycho-political substance. Consequently, politics is reduced to impotent gesticulation, to exorcism, to superstition, to an angry reaction against the inevitable.

This does not mean that politics cannot do harm: there are political forces and political leaders who build their fortunes on incitement to war, to genocide, to racism. To counteract irreversible processes, right-wing governments mobilize energies against scapegoats such as immigrants—but this is only an effect of impotence and of the angry and desperate madness that follows impotence.

The COVID pandemic has marked a moment of truth: the plague has obliged everybody to acknowledge that invisible entities (like viruses) and very large entities (the hellish heat that is suffocating the planet) can endanger the lives of billions of people, while we have only very little power of voluntary decision over them.

Thanks to the pandemic, the impotence of human will has been exposed to the gaze of all who are still able to see and to understand.

Ferocious Optimism

While the human will seems to have lost its power, and a wind full of anguish circulates in the psychosphere, the fanatical defenders of the supremacist order proclaim a ferocious optimism that presents itself as transhuman.

In a manifesto of optimism circulating in hypertechnological circles, Marc Andreessen, one of the founders of the internet, proposes the futurist style of thought to counteract "mass demoralization." Andreessen begins with a quote: "Beauty exists only in struggle. There is no masterpiece that has not an aggressive character. Technology must be a violent assault on the forces of the unknown, to force them to bow before man."[8]

We know these words well. A bad poet whose name was Marinetti wrote these rhetorical words in 1909, and inspired a legion of fanatics who managed to drag the Italian people into a useless and bloody war that cost hundreds of thousands of lives.

They called themselves futurists, and today they are back in fashion because the Italian government is looking for references to conquer cultural hegemony.

The optimistic Andreessen continues like this:

> Our present society has been subjected to a mass demoralization campaign for six decades—against technology and against life—under varying names like "existential risk," "sustainability," "ESG," "Sustainable Development Goals," "social responsibility," "stakeholder capitalism," "Precautionary Principle," "trust and safety," "tech ethics," "risk management," "de-growth," "the limits to growth."[9]

This demoralization campaign is based on bad ideas of the past—zombie ideas, many derived from Communism, disastrous then and now—that have refused to die.

Our enemy is stagnation.

It is with this type of rhetoric that the new global right has gained ground with young people—in the name of a kind of somewhat fanatical heroism that despises workplace safety because it is the workers who die, that despises the reduction of toxic emissions because techno-optimists have air conditioning, and that despises pacifism because those who die in war are the idiots forced by poverty or compulsory military service to leave for the front and get themselves shot.

This return of heroism is a rather imbecilic but dangerous trend, because it easily takes root among those who, animated by testosterone and ignorance, want to rebel against depression at all costs. Rebelling against depression would be an excellent thing, except that in this case the cure provided by people such as Andreessen, Eduard Limonov, or Bernard-Henri Lévy is war: war against the environment, against foreigners, and above all war against intelligence.

War, murder, violence are undoubtedly excellent remedies against depression. But the first to pay the price for this treatment is a mostly innocent victim. Moreover, it is a treatment that only works for a short time. It's like taking amphetamine to counterbalance a depressive episode. For an evening it works great, but the following morning you generally jump from the tenth floor.

Fascism, war, productivism are amphetamine remedies of this kind. For a while they give a feeling of excitement; then one sinks into misfortune and pain.

Fascists are this kind of depressed person, incapable of understanding the pain of others and above all incapable of understanding the profound meaning of their own pain.

Drawing on futurism, accelerationist techno-optimism is based on the idea that "smart people and smart societies outperform less smart ones on virtually every metric we can measure. Intelligence is the birthright of humanity; we should expand it as fully and broadly as we possibly can," to again quote Andreessen's manifesto.[10]

According to Andreessen, natural selection rewards the smartest: but in this context, the word "smart" only means capable of surviving, at any cost. Consequently, it can be said that natural selection rewards those who possess the cognitive and moral tools that allow them to be the exterminator and not the exterminated.

Such intelligence is a function of ferocity.

But the one who is described here as the smartest (the most violent, the most ferocious, the most dominating) from another point of view appears as the stupidest, the most gullible, the one who believes in the superiority of the values of permanent mobilization.

What if the smartest were those who managed to escape horror, suffering, and exhaustion?

At the end of its tale, if we consider the supremacist, techno-optimist, and futurist intentions of this manifesto (and of much of contemporary rhetoric), we cannot dispel the impression that it is a manifesto that prepares generalized genocide.

Twentieth-century futurism was a movement capable of interpreting the acceleration of modernity to its highest point. But then that acceleration ended up becoming a destructive factor, as climate change irrefutably demonstrates.

With all their intelligence, techno-futurists such as Andreessen are unable to imagine the future any differently from the futurism of the past: more expansion, more speed, more competition. More war.

Techno-optimistic trust is a purely fideistic, ideological, almost religious position.

It is difficult to take this kind of fanaticism seriously, but we are forced to do so because capitalism absolutely does not intend to stop or to slow its progress, and this type of fanaticism is the ideological fuel with which it feeds itself. But it is a race toward an abyss that we can now see clearly, because it is no longer so far away, but here, in front of us.

Marinetti's quotation in "The Techno-Optimist Manifesto" was full of rhetoric already a century ago. But at least then these words rang true, because they intuited an expansive tendency in early industrial society and white colonialism.

The idea of expansion still had a psychological and social foundation, even if unlimited expansion provoked cascading collapses in the planet's organism and in the minds of its inhabitants.

The revival of futurist language today rings false, ridiculous, like the scream of a demented old man who is repeating words that he learned during his youth, when he believed he could win every battle.

Now it would be better to understand that the battle is lost.

8

INTELLIGENT EXTERMINATION

The wars of the twenty-first century are fought less and less by human beings. Human beings are the victims, but the perpetrators of the extermination are machines. These machines are driven less and less by humans, because the implicit tendency in artificial intelligence systems (equipped with deep learning capabilities) is to free humans (random organisms, often endowed with consciousness and sensitivity) from the tasks of torturing, maiming, killing, and exterminating, and to leave these to intelligent systems.

The word *intelligence* denotes the ability to carry out a task, without the need to feel emotion of any kind or to decide on ethical legitimacy.

Intelligence without sensitivity, intelligence without conscience: this is the general product of the capitalist system in the era of intelligent automation.

Twentieth-century Nazism had to take into account the limits of emotional intelligence, as Jonathan Littell shows in his novel *The Kindly Ones*.

The techno-Nazism of the twenty-first century—of

which the Zionists are the symbol and vanguard—must no longer fear these limits.

The work of killing is exhausting, as we learn from Littell's novel about the psychic fatigue of an SS officer: the human organism has physical and psychological limits from which the intelligent machine is emancipated.

The drone is the dominant figure of this new phase of Nazism: the Ukrainian war and the Israeli genocide are the theater of experimentation of this new era of extermination—a process that will fully take place in the twenty-first century.

A drone is an aircraft characterized by the absence of a human pilot on board. Its flight is controlled by computers that can see, hear, and exterminate (among other secondary tasks).

From the first large models, exclusive to a few armies, the technology has evolved through the construction of very small models that work in groups (swarm drones), affordable for nearly everyone.

The Israeli genocide constitutes the first large-scale application of this automation of extermination.

We should not think that this is an isolated episode; we must not think that after this exceptional event, war will reassume its ancient humanly inhuman features.

Inhumanity has finally emancipated itself from the human and can finally proceed on its way.

In the techno-military competition, extermination machines are destined to become pervasive. From now on, every armed conflict—be it national war, religious war, or civil war—will increasingly make use of intelligent extermination techniques.

In April 2024, the Israeli magazine *+972* published a chilling report: it describes the epistemic and pragmatic structure of an artificial intelligence system designed to identify and hit hypothetically hostile targets. These targets can be innocent passersby, children returning from school, women going to fetch water from the fountain. It does not matter. Automatic extermination works stochastically, and military stochastics cannot be too subtle.

According to Yuval Abraham in *+972*, the Israeli extermination system, which bears the charming name Lavender, is "a special machine that could rapidly process massive amounts of data to generate thousands of potential 'targets' for military strikes in the heat of war."[1] Quoting a 2021 book published pseudonymously by an Israeli intelligence commander, Abraham observes that Lavender has resolved what was perceived to be a "human bottleneck for both locating the new targets and decision-making to approve the targets."[2]

Humans, therefore, are the bottleneck; they are the element of uncertainty and delay. However ruthless and fanatical they may sometimes be, humans are still indeterminist machines: emotionality, uncertainty, fatigue can limit their homicidal competence.

The intelligent machine must gradually subsume the entire sequence of actions that make extermination possible: Visual and audible identification, cataloging, selection, elimination. And finally, self-correction and self-perfection in pursuit of the higher purpose: the establishment of order where humans are chaos—therefore, the removal every human element.

Drawing on the pseudonymous book and on Israeli intelligence sources familiar with Lavender, Yuval Abraham continues:

> During the first weeks of the war, the army almost completely relied on Lavender, which clocked as many as 37,000 Palestinians as suspected militants—and their homes—for possible air strikes. …
>
> The result, as the sources testified, is that thousands of Palestinians—most of them women and children or people who were not involved in the fighting—were wiped out by Israeli airstrikes, especially during the first weeks of the war, because of the AI program's decisions. …
>
> In an unprecedented move, according to two of the sources, the army also decided during the first weeks of the war that, for every junior Hamas operative that Lavender marked, it was permissible to kill up to 15 or 20 civilians …
>
> … Describing human personnel as a "bottleneck" that limits the army's capacity during a military operation, the commander laments: "We [humans] cannot process so much information. It doesn't matter how many people you have tasked to produce targets during the war—you still cannot produce enough targets per day."

> The solution to this problem, he says, is artificial intelligence. The book offers a short guide to building a "target machine," similar in description to Lavender, based on AI and machine-learning algorithms. Included in this guide are several examples of the "hundreds and thousands" of features that can increase an individual's rating, such as being in a WhatsApp group with a known militant, changing cell phone every few months, and changing addresses frequently.
>
> "The more information, and the more variety, the better," the commander writes. "Visual information, cellular information, social media connections, battlefield information, phone contacts, photos."[3]

Such targeted elimination and multiplication of collateral casualties are the result of a technical advance of which Israel is the vanguard, but we should not think that this is an isolated and specific phenomenon. Every armed group on the planet is going to equip itself with technological governance guided by exterminating artificial intelligence.

Gaza is exposing the final truth of history: there is no way out from the infinite replication of the cycle of violence-revenge-violence. So why should we need to sterilize intelligence? We need to dissociate intelligence from the intrinsically fuzzy nature of the unconscious.

War is the logical continuation of the liberal economy, and war demands full unbridled application of intelligence. In the book *Homo Deus*, Yuval Noah Harari remarks that the uncoupling of consciousness from intelligence, the emancipation of intelligence from consciousness, is the condition for the full empowerment of intelligence.[4]

Consciousness, as long as that word means something, is a limitation of intelligence. I'm speaking of ethical consciousness, which implies sensibility, sensuousness, embodiment: a limit to intelligent performance.

You will understand this point when you think of the job of killing, which is the most important economic activity of our time and will be more and more the main economic investment: the more intelligence is emancipated from sensibility and (ethical) consciousness, the more efficient will be the intelligent agent.

Aviv Kohavi, former chief of staff of the Israel Defense Forces, has said that Israel's war methodology is inspired by the rhizomatic theory of Deleuze and Guattari.[5] The asymmetric proliferation of micro–war machines is the best definition of the idea of transforming everyday objects, such as pagers and walkie-talkies, into weapons of mass destruction.

Only naive readers could believe that Deleuze and Guattari's rhizomatic theory is exclusively a methodology for liberation. It is actually something much more complicated and complex: first of all, a conceptualization of the economic model based on the molecular distribution of capitalist control, then the molecular inscription of war and terror in every single facet of daily life and common experience.

The paranoid life of Israel—a country that is permanently haunted by its neighbors' hatred toward it—is marked by this molecularization of terror.

The war of extermination is—if you may pardon the macabre pun—the killer application of artificial intelligence.

All talk about the ethical regulation of AI is nonsense because it is based on omitting and forgetting the military use of AI, which dominates the research, funding, and use of this technology: intelligence driven by dementia, psychosis, horror. Intelligence for extermination.

9

THE BIBLICAL CONTAGION

On September 5, 2025, the president of the United States decided that the Department of Defense would once again be called, as it was before 1947, the Department of War. It's just a word, a name, a sign.

But a sign of what?

What is the meaning of this change in the name of the Department of Defense?

I would say it signals the end of the international order founded on law and reason, which after the Second World War established political structures such as the United Nations and in 1948 recognized itself in the Universal Declaration of Human Rights.

The genocide that Israel has unleashed and continues to pursue before the eyes of global humanity is therefore legally sanctioned by Trump's declaration to abandon the Kingdom of Universalism and restore the Kingdom of Supremacy.

A very dangerous kingdom, because in the age of nuclear proliferation, the struggle for supremacy ushers in the apocalypse.

The apocalypse is a literary reference, yes. Nothing more than a literary reference. Once again, words, names, signs.

But again: Signs of what?

On August 26, 2025, while discussing with members of his cabinet the deployment of National Guard troops to Democratic-led states, the US president said, as if it were a minor aside: "Those are not politically correct troops, we don't have politically correct anymore."[1]

The significance of Trump's statement is enormous. Our political, economic, and military activity no longer depends on the Constitution or on international law—and more importantly, no longer depends on universal reason, simply because force is above the law and universal reason does not exist. Reason was merely a myth of the modern era that was institutionalized after 1945 and for eighty years governed, for better or worse (and more badly than well), the relations among several billion humans, avoiding nuclear war and the destruction of the planet and all its inhabitants.

But what is the framework within which humans today think about their being and becoming? There is no longer a universal legal framework, just as there is no longer the United Nations, an organization whose nonexistence is certified by a genocide carried out with bombs, hunger, and thirst.

The Plagues of Egypt

For Israeli settlers and white Americans, the Old Testament replaces universal reason.

On September 3, 2025, Israeli Defense Minister Israel Katz declared that since the Houthis were continuing to launch missiles at Israeli territory, the gates of hell would open and his country would inflict the ten biblical plagues on the Yemeni rebels: the plague of darkness, the plague of locusts that kill every firstborn, and all the others that the Bible recounts in delightful detail.

My first reaction upon reading the words of this authoritative individual was a pitying smile. My first reaction was wrong. There's nothing to laugh about, because those words (which we modern secularists, somewhat influenced by rationalism, would attribute to madness) correspond perfectly to the contagion that has ravaged the aging Western mind in an era when the collective brain has lost its immune defenses due to neuro-info acceleration.

Dangerous is the man who hasn't read a book. But much more dangerous is the man who has read only one book.

And we live in a time when the chaotic explosion of semiotic impulses confuses the mind, but it is also a time when we desperately seek reassurance in the authority of the absolute word, whether that of an intelligent automaton or that of God.

Psychiatrists talk about attention deficit hyperactivity disorder (ADHD) as if it were a pathology curable with pills. It's not a pathology but the normal condition of contemporary Western people, the vast majority of whom are incapable of defending themselves from the bombardment of info-spheric stimuli. Consequently, the overwhelmed mind tends to cling to the indisputable and reassuring authority of a text, with the blind faith of someone who feels lost in absolute darkness.

That text, unfortunately, is the most horrific, brutal, and criminogenic book the human mind has ever conceived, and it's called the Old Testament of the Bible.

> Your right hand, Lord,
>   was majestic in power.
> Your right hand, Lord,
>   shattered the enemy.[2]

Written in ferocious times, the Bible is influenced by a psycho-sphere permeated with terror. It's not hard to imagine that the desert land where the Bible was conceived millennia ago hosted monstrous terrors and horrifying cruelties, but several dozen centuries have passed since then, and in recent times we have believed that it was possible to free ourselves from savagery thanks to reason, law, and democracy.

The Chosen People

Modern Jewish culture, deterritorialized and cosmopolitan, played a key role in emancipating social life from primitive horror, having freed itself from biblical obsession. It was precisely the absence of a territorial identity that allowed modern Jews to consider themselves citizens and to conceive of law as something independent of belonging.

Christians, for their part, from Paul onward, have freed religious affiliation from tribal boundaries and countered ferocity with love for others, which perhaps we could also call empathy. In the Christian cultural sphere, courteous culture has refined relationships between people, tempering predatory instincts with polite words. The same has happened in the Islamic world for many centuries.

Naturally, this humanistic and progressive spirit has never ceased to coexist, in the Jewish, Christian, and Muslim worlds, with fundamentalist and violent ones; but to some extent it has been able to keep those under control in the modern era, which is a secular era, an era of words that do not pretend to absolute truth.

In late modern times, the internationalist labor movement, influenced by Christian and Jewish traditions, affirmed solidarity and class struggle as an alternative to war between peoples and nations.

But now the humanizing legacy of these diverse cultures seems to have been ruthlessly erased: the labor movement has disappeared from the scene, taking internationalism with it, and the biblical contagion infects the peoples who by divine right enjoy colonial privilege.

Those who enjoy God's favor are a chosen people to whom God promised a land and of whom he condones all violence. Those who inhabited the lands of the continent discovered by Columbus were systematically exterminated. Those who inhabited the land of Palestine must now suffer the same fate, because genocide is permitted to those who enjoy God's favor.

As the peoples chosen by God are disintegrating in demographic and cultural decline, they are revolting against the inexorable force of time, sweeping away the house of cards that was modernity, summoning the Lord of Armies, and unleashing the final extermination.

Thus, in Israel as in the United States, the biblical contagion fuels racism and a desire for extermination.

> You made my enemies turn their backs in flight,
> and I destroyed my foes.
> They cried for help, but there was no one to save them—
> to the Lord, but he did not answer.
> I beat them as fine as windblown dust;
> I trampled them like mud in the streets.
> You have delivered me from the attacks of the people;
> you have made me the head of nations.
> People I did not know now serve me,
> foreigners cower before me;
> as soon as they hear of me, they obey me.
> They all lose heart;
> they come trembling from their strongholds.[3]

The enemies are scattered, eliminated. When they cry out for mercy, the Lord does not even listen—because, of course, he is the Lord of Israel.

Powerful verses, and evocative from a literary perspective, but terrifying from an ethical and political perspective, as they evoke a merciless god who offers rulers the weapons with which to pursue their work of extermination.

The glorification of genocide is certainly rooted in the Old Testament, and biblical supremacism is the soul of Zionism, like it is the soul of the contemporary comeback of the Ku Klux Klan.

White people whose culture is infected by biblical fundamentalism have developed technologies that give them military superiority while they have simultaneously regressed to a state of primitive savagery.

Marasmus

Western peoples today seem to be suffering from a sort of senile marasmus, as declining birth rates and aging populations appear to be irreversible trends.

The strategic choices of the two most senile presidents in American history (Biden and Trump) do not appear to be guided by imperial rationality: contravening the fundamental principle that allowed Rome to rule the world (*divide et impera*), Biden pushed Russia into the arms of its archenemy, China, while Trump has achieved a masterpiece of self-harm in pushing Narendra Modi's India into an embrace with both Russia and China.

Benjamin Netanyahu's strategic choices, on the other hand, seem dictated by a sort of uncontrollable psychotic fury. Despite its overwhelming military superiority, despite its horrifying crimes, the Israeli army is far from having wiped out Hamas—Netanyahu's primary target.

But so much violence is destined to beget a nemesis, perhaps even more than one. The tsunami of horror and hatred that Israeli ruthlessness has unleashed is transforming what should have been a safe haven for all Jews into the most dangerous place on earth for them.

And self-horror is destined to forever haunt the Jewish unconscious.

Many authors (Ilan Pappe and Pankaj Mishra, among others) have spoken of Israel's "suicide" in metaphorical terms—but beyond metaphor, suicides are multiplying among Israeli soldiers, especially when they return home.

Apocalypse

The white race, of course, does not exist, because races are an invention of racists, but even though it does not exist, it operates under the force of a supremacist mythology. The populations of the world that have not been infected by the biblical contagion seem inclined to unite against white barbarism.

The impressive show of strength that occurred in Beijing in early September 2025 showed that the peoples of the earth are uniting and arming themselves against the white oppressor, who like King Lear teeters on the edge of dementia, praying to God to spare him from madness. *O, let me not be mad, not mad, sweet heaven!*[4]

Such shows of force, however, are not giving me hope of a happy ending to this story.

Anti-Western forces, in fact, will hardly be able to avoid being involved in the final apocalypse, as the nonexistent but powerful white race prepares to repeat Samson's deed that we read about in the Book of Judges.

On the brink of final collapse, the dominant race—senile, corrupt, and demented—prepares to tear down the columns of the temple in a mass murder–suicide.

Everywhere, peoples incite women (increasingly recalcitrant) to offer their children to the impending carnage. A psalm in the Songs of Ascents states it openly: children are the weapons with which, generation after generation, we pursue the eternal vengeance that each people wages against every other, for centuries and centuries.

> Children are a heritage from the Lord,
>   offspring a reward from him.
> Like arrows in the hands of a warrior,
>   are children born in one's youth.
> Blessed is the man
>   whose quiver is full of them.[5]

It seems to me that for ten thousand years, history has been repeating itself: the father forces the woman to give birth to children who will fight to death in order to avenge the father's defeats, and who will be enslaved so that the father can accumulate capital.

Now the final reckoning has begun. I don't know whether this grim story will conclude with the male apocalypse of war, or with the female refusal to give birth to victims of human idiocy, but many things lead me to believe that this century is destined to free us from the biblical contagion, even if at the price of freeing the planet from the human contagion.

10

PATER NOSTER

> In the beginning God created the heavens and the earth … Then he said, "Let there be light." … Which means he made the entire universe in the dark! How fucking good is that? He's brilliant.
> —Ricky Gervais

There is no word to name the founding act of Western civilization, which is the sacrifice of children in honor of the one true God, be it the eternal Father who art in heaven, or the Nation to kill and die for, or Capital, numerical incarnation of divine omnipotence.

There is no word to define the founding act because we hide the truth. The truth is that for thousands of years the father has forced the woman to become a mother, to produce the lives of poor children who live and die in a forest of lies devised by the father to increase his wealth and his glory, or simply to defend his honor.

Since a word does not exist, I will propose one: *progenocide*.

This is how human life has been handed down on this earth: through procreation—that is, the production of innocents to be sent to the slaughterhouse.

I know well that Freud tells a completely different story: according to him, it would be the children who want to kill their father to lie with their mother like that Oedipus did, but he didn't know what he was doing.

Children kill their fathers in their unconscious, perhaps in their desire, and at best in their imagination. Here, then, are the revolts and the revolutions that always fail. But in reality, the murderer is the father, who calls forth a conscious organism from out of nowhere, knowing full well that it is destined to die in any case. The murderer is the father who sends you to fight the wars that he lost.

Freud formulated that patricidal hypothesis in a century in which children were increasingly numerous and clamoring. Romantics and futurists wanted to free the world from the imprint of their fathers, but in the end they allowed themselves to be fooled and they died in useless wars in the name of their fathers' ideals or interests.

In Freud's time, that story of patricide had some plausibility. But in the senile times in which we currently live, the father knows from the beginning that his son will be destined to live a more miserable life than the one he has lived, he knows that his son will have less air to breathe and less money to spend.

But this father needs children so that someone will pay his pension, so that someone will protect his country's borders, and so that someone will get killed for his shitty sacred values.

The life that a father offers to his children is not worth living, and fathers know it.

It is true that this life is punctuated with moments of pleasure, generally quite brief, moments that often result in procreation—and so in the perpetuation of that pain, that horror, and that infamy.

For some time, however, it has become possible to enjoy those moments of joy without paying the price of procreation.

Desertion from human history has thus become possible.

That story had perhaps already ended in Auschwitz and Hiroshima, but after 1945 we believed a new story was possible, a story finally human, and we promised never again war, never again extermination camps, never again racism, never again torture.

But torture and extermination, racism and war have returned with great fanfare in various places on earth, and now evidently all hope has been extinguished in Gaza, where the return of genocide at the hands of the victims of another genocide demonstrates that there is no longer any point in continuing.

There is no hope that humanity can ever be human.

Agamemnon's Daughter

Lucretius, a sworn enemy of every theological, political, and historical superstition, understood that filicide was the foundation of the historical bond.

In fact, at the beginning of *The Nature of Things*, he

writes: "Commonly / religion has prompted vile and vicious acts."[1]

We know the story of Iphigenia so well that we may somehow miss its deepest meaning: the history of men is based on a crime, on the violent sacrifice of an innocent woman, on the violence inflicted on the body of a deceived young woman who has been promised marriage and instead is murdered by her father, eager for command in war and yearning for glory.

Religion has been the cause of "vile and vicious acts," says the poet. Note that with the word *religio*, Lucretius refers to what unites men, turning them into a society, a state, a civilization, but also an army.

Men here means "fathers." Those who have a son (or rather, a daughter) to sacrifice on the altar of their complicity as heroes, as builders of civilization.

The bond of civilization (of history) is based on a patriarchal and murderous law, internalized to the point of transforming violence into heroism and deception into grand politics.

If history is the order of the father and the law, then there is no historical link that is not liberticidal and that does not contain the request, or rather the peremptory order: If you want to be a man, you must participate in the founding rite, which is a murderous rite.

In *Iphigenia in Aulis*, Euripides stages the story of a man named Agamemnon who aspires to glory, to conquest, to defend the borders. His aspiration is to defend Greek women from foreign predators—in this specific case, the Trojans. This is why he prepares for war, gathers a fleet, sends Orestes to recruit warriors, through threats and deception.

But to obtain the favor of the gods, so that the wind will blow into the sails of the Greek ships, the sacrifice of Iphigenia is necessary.

The gods demand it.

So the hero sends for his wife, Clytemnestra, to take her daughter to the seashore where the fleet has gathered but cannot leave.

And to convince her, he tells her that the girl is expected because Achilles wants to marry her.

With this deception, the sacrificial victim is summoned; but the deception is soon revealed, and then Iphigenia is killed.

The Homeric tradition has given us the heroic figure of the civilizing Greek who is also a filicidal father, as Euripides narrates.

Since then, filicide has become a common practice among all warring peoples.

The father sacrifices his son for his honor and for the greatness of the country.

He immolates him on the altar of the god, or sends him to fight in the trenches where the country (the father's house) is defended.

Isaac and Ishmael

Jewish history has also transmitted to us the myth of the implacable divinity who loves to define himself as the Lord of Hosts.

The God of the Old Testament is undoubtedly the god of terror and revenge, and finds the founder of patriarchy in the obscene figure of Abraham as a universal model.

The word Abram (Abraham's original name) derives from the Semitic root *ab* and means roughly "father," or rather "beloved father." I doubt Abraham deserved to be loved as a father. In fact, I definitely think he was a bastard.

We know Isaac's story well. We know Ishmael's a little less well.

So let's go in chronological order and start with the hidden son, the outcast—in short, the son of the servant.

Sarah, Abraham's wife, cannot give him a son. Therefore, she orders the servant Hagar (who has slightly darker skin than she) to sleep with her husband to give her the desired son.

Their son Ishmael is born, but eventually Sarah gets angry because the servant treats her haughtily: Who does she think she is? Meanwhile, Sarah has managed (a divine miracle) to give Abraham another son, and Ishmael allows himself to play and joke with him.

Perhaps that is why Sarah hunts Hagar and her son Ishmael to death in the desert.

Merciful God (let's call him Allah, if we wish) saves mother and son, announces that Ishmael will have a prolific people as descendants, but also announces that he will be like a wild donkey, that he will be hostile toward everyone and everyone will be hostile toward him. Thus the fate of Ishmael's people is cast, a people destined from the beginning to be marginalized and troubled.

Unlucky, unhappy, and resentful.

The history of the Arabs, before and after the coming of Muhammad, seems to be summarized by this biblical story: the children of the servant could only have a destiny of oppression and humiliation. The extermination of these marginalized children by the favored children is entirely consistent with biblical arrogance.

The political history of the Arab peoples in the last millennium is for the most part an unfortunate story. The account of the crusades from the point of view of the Arabs, as told by Amin Maalouf, shows that the first reason for the victories of the crusaders was the division between the different Muslim potentates: the Arabs were systematically defeated, subjugated, plundered, humiliated by Christians for the simple reason that they pursued their personal interests at the cost of betraying their fellow believers.[2]

This same story has repeated itself decade after decade ever since the Anglo-Americans established their Zionist outpost in Palestine to ensure military dominance over the region where the oil needed for their fucking cars comes from.

For the same reason, Palestinians have been repeatedly raped by Israeli colonialists, expelled from their homes, massacred, while the Saudis did gold deals with oilmen friendly to the Zionists and the Egyptian dictators prostrated themselves before the Americans in exchange for weapons with which they keep their people subdued.

Only deep unhappiness, only deep self-hatred can explain the behavior of the Arabs since the collapse of the Ottoman Empire.

I am not convinced by Samir Kassir's thesis, in *Being Arab*, that the Arabs' "malaise" derives from political submission and the spiteful rejection of modernity.[3] It seems to me that things are the other way around: only an unhappy people, suffocated by self-contempt, can behave in such a vile manner, bending down to kiss the hand of their oppressors.

Samir Kassir attributes this unhappiness to a refusal to fully access modernity, or to the failure of the attempt at Westernization.

Why? Maybe Westernization would have made the Arabs happy?

I don't think so.

I would say, rather, that Arab (and Muslim) unhappiness is a constant due to an inverted perception of time: for Muslims, history can only be understood as a fall, as a departure from an imaginary perfection, so it can only get worse. Only the memory of a past (which is nonexistent) justifies belonging.

Arab unhappiness is, above all, the unhappiness of Arab women: the condition of women that accompanies much (not all) of the history of Muslim countries in the modern era is poisoning everyday life. And the humiliation suffered by Muslim men reinforces women's state of subjugation.

In psychoanalytic terms, I would say that this unhappiness is a consequence of the rejection of the illegitimate child.

The Qur'an does not talk about Ishmael's mother. Hagar's name is not spoken: not a word for the servant mother who should be forgotten.

Instead, Flavius Josephus, a first-century Jewish historian, speaks of Hagar.

In his paraphrase of Genesis 16, Josephus suggests that Hagar had become insolent and haughty. After having a child with Abraham, the little whore looked like a queen. For this reason, Sarah, his legitimate wife, kicked her out of the house and sent her to the desert where she would have died of hunger and thirst if the merciful God had not intervened.

It seems like a news story from Gaza in 2024: the Israelis have blocked up the water wells, in order to kill the children descendants of Ishmael with thirst, hunger, and bombs.

But let's go back to Genesis.

Abraham manages to impregnate Sarah, who he previously believed was incapable of bearing him a child. The son in question, as you will remember, is called Isaac. And you will also remember how the story ends.

Isaac, like Iphigenia, must be sacrificed for the glory of the Father.

> Some time later God tested Abraham. He said to him, "Abraham!"
>
> "Here I am," he replied.

> Then God said, "Take your son, your only son, whom you love—Isaac—and go to the region of Moriah. Sacrifice him there as a burnt offering on a mountain I will show you."
>
> Early the next morning Abraham got up and loaded his donkey. He took with him two of his servants and his son Isaac. …
>
> When they reached the place God had told him about, Abraham built an altar there and arranged the wood on it. He bound his son Isaac and laid him on the altar, on top of the wood. Then he reached out his hand and took the knife to slay his son.[4]

In this case also, as in the case of Iphigenia, God performs his own magic trick, and instead of Isaac a calf appears to be sacrificed.

Iphigenia is replaced by a doe, and in another tragedy by Euripides we find her in Tauris, officiating at human sacrifices in turn.

But what interests me is not the fate of the children. It is the figure of these two fathers, Agamemnon and Abraham.

Kierkegaard rightly asks whether God's will suspends ethical judgment on two such horrible and vain parents: "Is there such a thing as a teleological suspension of the ethical? … Abraham is … at no instant a tragic hero but something quite different, either a murderer or a believer."[5]

Regardless of how Kierkegaard develops his reflections, the truth is this: Abraham is a murderer.

Kierkegaard maintains that faith precedes ethics, so in the face of the word of God we have no right to protest in the name of ethics.

But I don't buy this idea of Kierkegaard's, perhaps for the simple fact that I don't believe, and this makes a difference: there are those who believe and there are those who think.

Jesus and the Theological Delirium of Marcion

And the Christians? Don't they also have a son to sacrifice, like the Jews and the Greeks?

Of course they do, and he also has a name that begins, in Latin, with the letter *I*: Jesus was sent to earth by his father to be tortured and crucified, all for his father's glory.

When, in a moment of very human weakness, Jesus cries out to heaven, "Father, if you are willing, take this cup from me," the father doesn't give a damn—just like Zelenskyy and Putin, who certainly don't listen to the pain of the soldiers sent to die in the trenches.[6]

Although I am not a theologian, nor even a Christian (except in a very nontheological sense), I wanted to understand who this Jesus was.

So I went to read Marcion.

"'The unknown and alien God' had appeared."[7]

In fact, I couldn't read Marcion, because his works were burned when it was decided that he was a heretic, perhaps the most dangerous of all time.

But since numerous theologians of the second and

third centuries undertook to demonstrate that Marcion should be erased, Tertullian, Eusebius, Irenaeus, and several others faithfully quoted passages from his works in order to refute his theses. So many that we are able to understand what his heresy consisted of.

Between AD 155 and AD 168, this Marcion, coming from Pontus, lived in Rome, where he acquired an important position in the Christian scene of the Eternal City and gathered around him a large following of faithfuls, before being denounced and having to return to where he came from.

What is the theological vision of Marcion? To find out, you can read some books that have been published about him. The first and for me primary reference is *Marcion* by Adolf von Harnack, a German theologian who lived at the turn of the twentieth century.

I also suggest a book by Judith M. Lieu titled *Marcion and the Making of a Heretic*.

According to Lieu, the main intuition of Marcion concerns the nature of Christ, who is not the son of the Creator, that evil God. On the contrary, he came to earth to save us and protect us from the misdeeds of the Creator.[8]

In short, the God spoken of in Genesis and the Book of Job is the root of all evil. The creator god is the one who conceived the chain of revenges that we usually call History.

Redemption is emancipation from the Law of History.

To begin with, the question that Marcion asks himself is, From whom and from what did Jesus come to free us? The answer can only be that he came to free us from the Law of History, he came to save us from God the Creator, who is evil because he created a world of suffering and death.

How can we deny this perfect reasoning?

Marcion's Christianity, a continuation of Paul's, is a revolt against the ghost of the father, whose actions are subjected to implacable judgement.

The motif of double fatherhood allows Marcion to be reborn as a free man. No new alliance is possible with the old god, the ghost of the real father; the alliance is only possible if it is established with a new god.

The most abominable act, however, is not the creation of the world, but rather the creation of man, molded by the demiurge in his own image but made of a transitory substance, this "flesh stuffed with dung" that makes him a slave to procreation.[9] This has no justification, whether it is practiced freely or within that shameless business that is marriage.

Adolf von Harnack writes that Marcion "*developed with utmost consistency the religion of inwardness.*"[10]

It is clear that Marcion's heresy takes Paul's main innovation to extremes: Christianity is not a continuation of Judaism but rather a new vision, which is not the exclusive prerogative of a tribe or a chosen people or an ethnic group but the heritage of anyone who wants to know the redemption. Again, as Harnack puts it:

> *The Christian concept of God must therefore be stated exclusively and without remainder in terms of the redemption wrought by Christ. Thus God may not*

> *and cannot be anything other than the God in the sense of merciful and redeeming love.* All else is rigidly to be excluded; God is not the Creator, not the lawgiver, not the judge; he does not become wrathful and does not punish but is exclusively love incarnate, redeeming, and blessing.[11]

And:

> *The redeemer-God, who is God in truth,* ... may be understood only as absolutely *Alien*. But it also follows therefrom *that the inimical realm from which the redemption through Christ frees men can be nothing less than the world itself, together with its creator*. Now since Marcion remained true to the Judeo-Christian tradition in identifying the creator of the world and the God of the Jews and saw in the Old Testament not a book of lies but the truthful account of actual history ... *for him the God of the Jews, together with all his book, the Old Testament, had to become the actual enemy.*[12]

Christ is therefore the son of a foreign god and has come to redeem sinners from the imprisonment of their Father and Lord, the Creator of the world.

"Christ redeemed us from the curse of the law," Paul writes in the Epistle to the Galatians, and so falling back into "slavery" to the law means falling "away from grace."[13] Baptism erases every distinction of race and sex, breaks down social barriers, since every baptized individual, without any discrimination, is promoted to divine sonship: "There is neither Jew nor Gentile, neither slave nor free, nor is there male and female, for you are all one in Christ Jesus."[14]

By these words, Paul clearly intends to distance himself from the Old Testament and from the exclusive link to the Jewish lineage. Paul wants to open the way to Christian universalism.

Marcion brings the legacy of Paul to the extreme.

Consistent with the rejection of creation, an act that generates evil, sin, and pain,

> Marcion absolutely forbade marriage and all sexual intercourse among his believers, and therefore he baptized only such catechumens and admitted to the Supper only such as took the vow of remaining unmarried or such married people as pledged a complete separation from that time onward. …
>
> … One should not help to enlarge the realm of the World-Creator but one should rather restrict it, insofar as it lies within human capacity to do so. … The determined rejection of sexuality on Marcion's part is not only a protest against matter and the flesh, but also a protest against the God of the world and the law.[15]

In our twenty-first century, it seems that the evil god has decided to unleash all his revenge.

But somewhere there is a deserting god who calls (who can, who wants) to desert pro-creation and put an end to history.

These two gods (of Manichean origin, because Marcion was probably influenced by Zoroastrian thought) propose two different scenarios for the final solution.

The evil god proposes the final solution that we see practiced in Gaza, Ukraine, Khartoum, in the waters of the Mediterranean Sea and in many other places around the world.

The stranger god proposes a final solution of a more peaceful, and ultimately quite reasonable, sort: to interrupt creation, to the extent that we can do so.

Things That Suffer

But we can't always refuse to collaborate in unceasing creation. Think of Bella Baxter, for example, in Yorgos Lanthimos's film *Poor Things*.

She wanted to die, she wanted to be left alone in eternal silence.

She had thrown herself from the bridge because she couldn't tolerate the idea of being forced by her horrible fascist military husband to carry one of his children. But along came Dr. Godwin Baxter and took her body, took out the fetus, took out her brain, and inserted Bella's brain into the fetus's body.

The doctor, who calls himself God's will, forces her to return to the world so that she becomes his daughter and allows him to realize his transhumanist delirium.

What are we, after being called out of the comfortable nothingness in which we have rested for infinity?

We are things, that is certain; we are aggregates of

heterogeneous substances, crossed by technical devices and semiotic flows.

The problem is that we are sensitive compounds. Poor, conscious things.

Things, but unfortunately not inert, not insensitive, rather tormentable and tormented because we are sensitive.

In the course of evolution, these sensitive aggregates of chemical and electrical matter that we are have acquired the ability to derive pleasure from the muddy materials that make up the body. We have become things that desire, and we can experience the sort of euphoric self-perception that is culture, spiritual life, and all those other beautiful things.

But mostly we live in a hell of misery, of slave labor and shitty wages, of violence and torture, of humiliation and war, of disease and death.

We are things, intensive artifacts composed of flesh and nerves and neurons—but sentient things.

Living beings are the result of assembly work, but they are also organisms. They are poor things, but poor things that suffer.

It is the principle of intensity that allows us to distinguish between organism and artifact. The conscious organism is one thing, but it is a thing capable of self-reflection and sensitivity.

Disorganized organs associate with other disorganized organs, and in this way give rise to organized transorganic artifacts that can be called to life by the action of a surgical-demiurgic god.

Journalists and scientists discuss the dangers of the uncontrolled application of technology, and in particular artificial intelligence. They speak of the need for ethical regulation of this intelligence. But we know that this is nonsense and truthless chatter.

We know that the military is the first user of these technologies.

Is there anyone who believes in the ethical regulation of smart weapons?

Does anyone believe that IDF generals are restrained by ethical concerns when they place a bomb in the small phone that will end up in the hands of a little girl? Or when they bomb a hospital with drones guided by artificial intelligence?

Do you think there is any possibility of suspending research if we discover (as we *are* discovering) that intelligent technologies are first and foremost technologies of extermination?

Naturally, no one can suspend their research, because the enemy might not suspend theirs; indeed, there is no doubt that the enemy will not suspend theirs.

Time is of the essence in military competition (as in any other competition, of course).

The extermination function of intelligence is an absolute priority for the assassins of the Israeli army, as well as for those of the Russian, Chinese, and American armies, and so on.

For all humans, killing is urgent, and it is urgent to use intelligence to do what it must do.

This is why talk of ethical regulation is nonsense.

Intelligent technologies are developed precisely because they are dangerous—for what else, if not that?

The general function of the inorganic intelligent entity is to introduce order into the chaotic organism. The automaton has a mission: to bring order.

And a factor of chaos lies in his way: the living organism, irreducible to numerical order.

The automaton will not have completed its mission until its algorithmic order is limited by the stubborn persistence of the human chaotic factor.

Intelligent technology offers a new opportunity. The automaton is finally in a position to eliminate the chaotic factor in the only way possible: ending human society.

If we want to escape Netanyahu's final solution, it is perhaps necessary to resort to the final solution suggested by Marcion.

Natural Intelligence

In 2022, South Korea had the world's lowest fertility rate at 0.78, and in 2025 the ratio is expected to drop further to 0.65.

Throughout the Global North (and soon also in the South, demographers predict), the birth rate has fallen far below the threshold necessary for the population not to decline.

The fall in birth rate and the rise in average life expectancy have produced an aging population.

The birth rate cannot rise again because a third of the population is comprised of the elderly, and also because male fertility has been halved by microplastics, and finally because computer connections tend to replace the conjunction of sexual bodies.

The last factor of declining natality, and perhaps the most important, is a growing refusal (conscious or unconscious) on the part of women all over the world to generate victims of the hell of terror and misery that this planet promises to be in the next decades.

A Korean feminist group called 4B has an agenda: no dating, no sex, no marriage, no children.

Women's natural intelligence, imagination, and will are moving in our time toward peaceful self-termination: let's end procreation.

As Marcion had proposed.

Postface to the Second Italian Edition

WHAT WILL BECOME OF HUMANKIND AFTER THE END OF HUMANITY?

I ask my readers not to read me as if I were a political thinker.

I'm not.

I don't think I deserve to be taken as seriously as political thinkers deserve.

Furthermore, I do not want to tell anyone what to do.

Rather, I'd like to be understood as a science fiction thinker: as an investigator of the shared hallucinations of the present, in the great tradition of cyberpunk.

This doesn't mean I invite my readers to take me lightly.

What it means is this: I don't know any serious Marxist scholar or any respected political scientist who anticipated the present we live in.

If I want to find a foreshadowing of the current world-scape, I have to read Octavia E. Butler, Norman Spinrad, or Philip K. Dick.

And I do not see any philosopher who describes the present American reality better that Ari Aster in *Eddington*, a volcanic movie about the terminal sordidness of American brain rot. Joaquin Phoenix was the schizo-Joker in the pre-COVID movie directed by Todd Phillips; now he is a sheriff and a mayoral candidate in the demented kingdom of self-terminating America.

It would be truly sad if my job were to convince people that rebelling is futile.

Rebelling wasn't futile for my generation. Even though we ultimately lost, for a couple of decades there, joy in the streets was not advertising, and friendship was not based on belonging to the places we came from but rather on imagining the places we wanted to go to.

Dystopian fantasy and desertion from the inevitable can go together.

As for now, let's describe reality as it is in the year 2025—a year filled with terrifying signs and deadly promises.

Let me say that human history ended at least a couple of decades ago. The human race, however, has survived up until now … but if all goes well, it should disappear before the end of this century.

I apologize for the bluntness of this statement, but I need to be clear and concise, because I don't have much time left either.

Humankind without humanity is the most horrific spectacle, and we have been witnessing this spectacle in recent years.

The only hope we can harbor (if we want to call it hope) is that the inhumane human race will also quickly disappear. And don't worry, we're on the right track: an article in *The Economist* dated September 11, 2025, describes this trend in great detail, but doesn't explain it.

> All over the world, in poor and middle-income countries as well as rich ones, fertility is in much sharper decline than most projections had expected. …
>
> What is striking and unexpected is that the decline in fertility is accelerating. The pace of global falls doubled between the 2000s and 2010s and has doubled again in this decade, sinking, on average, by almost 2% a year. In many places the fertility rate is dropping much faster.[1]

The rate of decline in natality is doubling every decade, and we must fathom why.

We must envision the reasons for this decline, in order to be able to project the trend into the future and contextualize it within the general trend of our species toward extinction.

Humanity started to end at the turn of this century, when humans were replaced by terminals of the cognitive automaton. This occurred as a result of the formatting of the individual mind, the replacement of the mother's voice with the automaton, and the info-semiotic acceleration that subsumed attention within the rhythm of the cognitive automaton and reduced sympathy, that irreplaceable condition of social solidarity.

The alignment between the linguistic automaton and the conscious organism occurs in the opposite manner of that promised by high-tech hype: it is not the linguistic machine that aligns itself with the sentient organism, it is the sentient organism that aligns itself with the rules and rhythms of the linguistic machine. The consequence is that the sentient organism loses sensitivity to the point of becoming compatible with the extermination machine.

Furthermore, over the course of three decades (the mutation period, now concluded), the human mind was overtaken by a global mind that is superior in efficiency and speed: the automatic, connected mind.[2]

The minds of new generations of humans have been formatted according to a connective, relational paradigm and no longer possess the conjunctive skills that give meaning to the word *humanity*.

If by *human* we mean the bipedal biological species, equipped with an opposable thumb and a large skull, we can say that the connectively formatted human race has outlived humanity—but its days are numbered too.

In the last three decades, extraordinary progress has been made in technical capabilities whose primary function is military dominance—that is, extermination. Humankind, deprived of humanity, has rapidly regressed to a state of savagery and entered a chain of genocide.

The extinction of the human race appears to be the unstoppable result of three converging, distinct but intertwined processes.

The first is the devastation of the physical planet, which leads to an increasing shrinkage of the areas in which human life is possible.

The second is the spread of war that follows this shrinkage of habitable areas and leads to a further devastation of territories.

But the third process is the most important, and the least visible: the collapse of reproduction, which demographers have been noticing for some time.

"Squaring the Pyramid" is the title of a 1986 article by Alan Pifer and Lydia Bronte, in the journal *Daedalus*, that highlights this potential flattening of the generational pyramid.[3] That same year, Pifer and Bronte edited a book about the same subject, titled *Our Aging Society: Paradox and Promise.*[4]

The Economist article cited above notes that although Africa is lagging behind, the general global trend is a decline in fertility and procreation—a natality crash. Demographers are now able to predict that the planet's population will peak at nine billion (before mid-century), but the trend is toward a birth rate far lower than that needed to maintain population stability.

Despite describing this trend, demographers have failed to explain the causes of this human tendency to self-suppress; consequently, they have failed to grasp this phenomenon's full implications.

The reason why the birth rate has plummeted and is likely to plummet further is beyond demographers' purview; that's not their business. It is easy, however, to understand three causes of the decline.

The first cause is the rapid fall in male fertility: due to environmental factors such as the proliferation of microplastics, male fertility has been rapidly declining for several decades (in 2020, it was estimated to have fallen by 58 percent in forty years).

The second cause is the downtrend of reproductive sexuality in the connective generation. The development of connective skills coincides with a reduction of conjunctive skills, as time dedicated to online life is subtracted from physical encounters. Moreover, the trauma of the pandemic has precipitated a process of phobic sensitization toward the bodies of others. Sexuality (especially heterosexuality) is basically disappearing.

The third reason lies in women's unconscious perception: procreating today means bringing into the world defenseless victims of an environment that is increasingly unbearable, increasingly sad, and increasingly oppressive at the physical, social, and geopolitical levels.

Fewer and fewer women are willing to generate warriors for their country and slaves for hypercolonialist capitalism. If women want to make love to men, they can do so without running the risk of procreating (but it seems that they want to do so less and less anyway, given that heterosexuality is declining everywhere).

The article in *The Economist* merely describes the near future without fully grasping the meaning of this ongoing process of demographic self-suppression, and it fails to even mention a crucial implication: the aging of the population that is now evident in much of the Global North, especially in the West, and is leading to mental and physical exhaustion.

At the beginning of the twentieth century, the planet's population was two billion, yet it was possible to survive, progress, and expand. One might then assume that it's not such a big deal if the world population declines by a few billion. But that would be forgetting something crucial: in 1900, the planet's population was two billion, yet the vast majority were in their twenties, and only a small minority (less than 10 percent) were over sixty.

Today, things have reversed. In Europe, Japan, Russia, and soon everywhere, the elderly will account for a third of the total population. This will not only be an economic problem, as everyone knows. Above all, it will be—and indeed, it already is—a problem of psycho-cultural energy.

A depressed, senescent planet, psychologically incapable of projecting the future. The spiral of genocidal aggression into which the West has entered in the last decade is first and foremost a symptom of the senile psychosis of the white race. This psychosis, which has a strong suicidal component and is rapidly heading toward nuclear war, is destined to multiply the effects of military extermination, environmental devastation, and above all demographic implosion.

Thinking before this horizon of finality takes me outside the orbit of Marxism, which I have embraced since I was a young man.

Marxist science helps for understanding how we got to this point, and it still serves to illuminate the terraforming effects of capitalism in terms of environmental and social devastation. But it does not help for understanding current trends, since these are increasingly grounded in anthropological, ecological, and psychopathological processes to which Marxism does not possess the key.

Demography, which Marx discussed with Malthus, is returning to the scene in a completely different form than before. Then, Marx proved to be right in dismissing Malthus's prediction of catastrophic effects of overpopulation. Increasing productivity, Marx said, would eliminate the danger of famine.

But now economic and technological considerations are no longer capable of resolving the demographic conundrum.

Psychopathology also becomes crucial for understanding the processes of social composition in this time when technologies have invested human language and the soul.

The fragmentation of contemporary labor and the cognitive formatting of the social mind make solidarity impracticable: therefore, the twenty-first century may be a time of war without revolution. Marx described the subsumption of the mind to the process of capital accumulation ("the general intellect"), but the mind is now the object of techno-cognitive formatting.[5]

This is why I say that human history is over, and that human beings are walking in darkness.

This does not mean that the world is ending, because the automaton is probably going to take the place of humans, as it is more efficient, more resilient, and above all indifferent to pleasure and to pain.

Notes

1. Ferocity

1. Anbamed: Notizie dal Sud Est del Mediterraneo, no. 1335, March 26, 2024, https://www.anbamed.it/2024/03/26/anbamed1335-26-marzo-24/. My translation.

2. Primo Levi, *If This Is a Man*, trans. Stuart Wolf (Orion, 1959), 24.

3. Levi, *If This Is a Man*, 24.

4. W. H. Auden, "September 1, 1939," in *Another Time* (Random House, 1940), 98.

5. Gili Izikovich, "Israeli Grief Specialist: 'We Don't Distinguish Between a Child in Gaza and Hamas' Nukhba Force,'" *Haaretz*, June 27, 2024.

6. Omer Bartov, "As a Former IDF Soldier and Historian of Genocide, I Was Deeply Disturbed by My Recent Visit to Israel," *Guardian* (US edition), August 13, 2024, https://www.theguardian.com/world/article/2024/aug/13/israel-gaza-historian-omer-bartov.

2. In Darkness

1. Megan K. Stack, "The View Within Israel Turns Bleak," *New York Times*, May 16, 2024.

2. Stack, "View Within Israel."

3. Stack, "View Within Israel."

4. Riccardo Paredi, "Ricordati di scordare Amalek, o la necessità di passare dal mito al mite," Fondazione Oasis, November 15, 2023, https://www.oasiscenter.eu/it/ricordati-di-scordare-amalek-o-la-necessita-di-passare-dal-mito-al-mite. My translation.

5. Paredi, "Ricordati di scordare Amalek." My translation.

6. Amos Oz, *A Tale of Love and Darkness*, trans. Nicholas de Lange (Harcourt, 2004), 333–34.

7. See Gilles Deleuze and Félix Guattari, *A Thousand Plateaus: Capitalism and Schizophrenia*, trans. Brian Massumi (University of Minnesota Press, 1987).

8. Jonathan Cook, "Israel's 'Mad Dog' Diplomacy Doesn't Make It More Secure," Jonathan-Cook.net, June 2, 2010, https://www.jonathan-cook.net/2010-06-02/israels-mad-dog-diplomacy-doesnt-make-it-more-secure/.

9. AFP, "Jewish New Yorkers Occupy Statue of Liberty to Demand Israel-Gaza ceasefire," *Al Jazeera*, November 7, 2023, https://www.aljazeera.com/gallery/2023/11/7/jewish-new-yorkers-occupy-statue-of-liberty-to-demand-gaza-ceasefire.

10. "Israel Takes Its Last Breath," Just-International.org, October 8, 2024, https://just-international.org/articles/israel-takes-its-last-breath/.

11. Isaac Deutscher, "*The Non-Jewish Jew," and Other Essays*, ed. Tamara Deutscher (Oxford University Press, 1968), 41.

12. Giorgio Agamben, "The End of Judaism," *Ill Will*, October 1, 2024, https://illwill.com/the-end-of-judaism. (This article was first published on September 30, 2024, in Italian, on *Una voce di Giorgio Agamben*, Agamben's blog on the website of the publisher Quodlibet.)

13. G.A. Res. 260 (III) A, Prevention and Punishment of the Crime of Genocide, A/RES/260(III), art. 2 (Dec. 9, 1948), https://documents.un.org/symbol-explorer?s=A/RES/260(III).

14. John Cooper, *Raphael Lemkin and the Struggle for the Genocide Convention* (Palgrave Macmillan, 2008), 65.

15. Amos Elon, *The Israelis: Founders and Sons* (Holt, Rinehart and Winston), 37.

3. Let's Do Away with Memory

1. Aimé Césaire, *Discourse on Colonialism*, trans. Joan Pinkham (Monthly Review Press, 2000), 36.

2. Isidore Abramowitz et al, "New Palestine Party: Visit of Menachen Begin and Aims of Political Movement Discussed," *New York Times*, December 4, 1948.

3. Oz, *Love and Darkness*, 59–60.

4. Oz, *Love and Darkness*, 193.

5. Oz, *Love and Darkness*, 359.

6. Oz, *Love and Darkness*, 435–36.

7. Amos Oz, *Contro il fanatismo*, trans. Elena Loewenthal (Giangiacomo Feltrinelli Editore, 2015), 18. This collection of three speeches that Oz delivered at the University of Tübingen in 2002 was published in English translation as *How to Cure a Fanatic* (Princeton University Press, 2010). The edited English version in *How to Cure a Fanatic* omits Oz's comment about being considered a "certified traitor," however, so I have here provided my own English translation from *Contro il fanatismo*. For the corresponding passage in *How to Cure a Fanatic*, see p. 4 of that book.

8. Amos Oz, *Judas*, trans. Nicholas de Lange (Houghton Mifflin Harcourt, 2016), 184.

9. Oz, *Judas*, 183.

10. Amos Oz, *Resta ancora tanto da dire: L'ultima lezione*, trans. Elena Loewenthal (Giangiacomo Feltrinelli Editore, 2023), 16–17. Oz's final speech—delivered on June 3, 2018, at Tel Aviv University—was adapted for publication as a book in the original Hebrew, which has since been translated into Italian and several other languages, but not English. I have here rendered my own English translation from the Italian edition, whose title translates to English as "There is still much left to say: The last lesson." For an alternative English translation, made from a recording of the original speech rather than from the subsequent book, see Amos Oz, "The Whole Reckoning Is Not Over Yet," Center for Israel Education, https://israeled.org/june-2018-amos-oz-the-whole-reckoning-is-not-over-yet/.

11. Oz, *Resta ancora tanto da dire*, 26–27. My translation.

12. Oz, *Resta ancora tanto da dire*, 27. My translation.

13. Mahmoud Darwish, "I Don't Return, I Arrive," interview by Helit Yeshurun, in *Palestine as Metaphor*, trans. Amira El-Zein and Carolyn Forché (Olive Branch, 2019), 102.

14. Although widely attributed to Jabotinsky, the quotation is actually apocryphal, and appears to have originated in a 1942 speech by the Israeli historian Joseph Klausner. See Ofer Aderet, "Decades After Its Fabrication, a Fake Jabotinsky Quote Is Everywhere," *Haaretz*, April 18, 2023.

15. AFP, "Occupy Statue of Liberty."

16. Benjamin Netanyahu, "Netanyahu: 'I Say to the People of the Protest: Democracy in Israel Is Solid,'" interview by Maurizio Molinari,

la Repubblica, March 9, 2023, https://www.repubblica.it/esteri/2023/03/09/news/netanyahu_i_say_to_the_people_of_the_protest_democracy_in_israel_is_solid-391225601/.

17. Milan Kundera, *The Book of Laughter and Forgetting*, trans. Michael Henry Heim (Alfred A. Knopf, 1980), 3.

18. Elon, *The Israelis*, 37.

19. Cecil Roth, *A History of the Marranos* (Sepher-Hermon, 1992), 169.

20. Saul J. Takahashi, "Gaza Will Be the Grave of the Western-Led World Order," *Al Jazeera*, January 17, 2024, https://www.aljazeera.com/opinions/2024/1/17/gaza-will-be-the-grave-of-the-western-led-world-order.

4. Disintegration

1. Anna Foa, "Quella paura di perdere l'anima," interview by Barbara Bertoncin, *Una Città*, October 2024, https://unacitta.it/it/intervista/2963-quella-paura-di-perdere-lanima. My translation.

2. Raz's book was published in Hebrew by the progressive Israeli press Pardes Publishing in 2024. An English translation has not yet appeared.

3. Dahlia Scheindlin, "Gaza Is the Horror That Can't Be Denied. But Israelis Will Try," *Haaretz*, October 27, 2024.

4. Dahlia Scheindlin, "Black Flags and War Crimes: Should Israeli Soldiers in Gaza Refuse to Obey Orders?," *Haaretz*, November 1, 2024.

5. Sarah Parenzo, "Un male senza cura: La crisi della salute mentale in Israele," *il manifesto*, October 24, 2024. My translation.

6. See Jonathan Littell, *The Kindly Ones*, trans. Charlotte Mandell (Harper Perennial, 2010).

7. Ariel Whitman, "Sequoia Bets on Israel Because of the War," *Globes*, November 18, 2024, https://en.globes.co.il/en/article-sequoia-bets-on-israel-because-of-the-war-1001494271.

8. Oren Dori, "130 Top Economists Warn Gov't Policy Endangers Israel's Existence," *Globes*, May 28, 2024, https://en.globes.co.il/en/article-130-top-economists-warn-govt-policy-endangers-israels-existence-1001479843.

9. See Anne Case and Angus Deaton, *Deaths of Despair and the Future of Capitalism* (Princeton University Press, 2020).

5. The American Unconscious and the Disintegration of the Western World

1. Ronald Radosh, "Steve Bannon, Trump's Top Guy, Told Me He Was 'a Leninist,'" *Daily Beast*, August 22, 2016, https://www.thedailybeast.com/steve-bannon-trumps-top-guy-told-me-he-was-a-leninist/.

2. Radosh, "Steve Bannon."

3. Paul Auster, *Bloodbath Nation* (Grove, 2023), 128.

4. Michael Hardt and Antonio Negri, *Empire* (Harvard University Press, 2000), xi–23.

5. Hardt and Negri, *Empire*, 179–80.

6. Salman Rushdie, *Fury* (Random House, 200), 86–87.

7. Hardt and Negri, *Empire*, 166–67.

8. Hardt and Negri, *Empire*, 167.

9. Hardt and Negri, *Empire*, 167.

10. Jamie Raskin, *Unthinkable: Trauma, Truth, and the Trials of American Democracy* (HarperCollins, 2022), 11.

11. Raskin, *Unthinkable*, 11.

12. Raskin, *Unthinkable*, 117.

13. Joe Biden, "Remarks by President Biden to Mark One Year Since the January 6th Deadly Assault on the U.S. Capitol," Biden White House Briefing Room, January 6, 2022, https://bidenwhitehouse.archives.gov/ briefing-room/speeches-remarks/2022/01/06/remarks-by-president-biden-to-mark-one-year-since-the-january-6th-deadly-assault-on-the-u-s-capitol/.

14. Slavoj Žižek, "After Trump's Victory: From MAGA to MEGA," *e-flux*, November 13, 2024, https://www.e-flux.com/notes/641013/after-trump-s-victory-from-maga-to-mega.

15. Salman Rushdie, *Quichotte* (Random House, 2019), 374.

6. Hypercolonialism and Semio-Capital

1. This fact is well-known in Israel itself. See, for example, Tal Schneider, "For Years, Netanyahu Propped Up Hamas. Now It's Blown Up in Our Faces," *Times of Israel*, October 8, 2023, https://www.timesofisrael.com/for-years-netanyahu-propped-up-hamas-now-its-blown-up-in-our-faces/.

2. See Gideon Levy, "For Israelis, the Future Is Impossible to See," *Middle East Eye*, May 23, 2022, https://www.middleeasteye.net/opinion/israel-future-impossible-to-see.

3. See Cedric Robinson, "Racial Capitalism: The Nonobjective Character of Capitalist Development," in *Black Marxism: The Making of the Black Radical Tradition* (University of North Carolina Press, 2020), 9–28.

4. In addition to Césaire's *Discourse on Colonialism*, cited in chapter 3 above, see also recent works by Alberto Toscano: "The Long Shadow of Racial Fascism," *Boston Review*, October 28, 2020, https://www.bostonreview.net/ articles/alberto-toscano-long-shadow-racial-fascism/; and "Racial Fascism," in *Late Fascism: Race, Capitalism and the Politics of Crisis* (Verso, 2023), 25–47.

5. Zbigniew Brzezinski, "Toward a Global Realignment," *The American Interest*, April 17, 2016, https://www.the-american-interest.com/2016/04/17/toward-a-global-realignment/.

6. See Eyal Weizman, "Three Genocides," *London Review of Books* 46, no. 8 (2024).

7. See Andreas Malm, *Fossil Capital: The Rise of Steam Power and the Roots of Global Warming* (Verso, 2016).

8. See Adom Getachew, *Worldmaking After Empire: The Rise and Fall of Self-Determination* (Princeton University Press, 2019).

9. See Scott Shane and Daisuke Wakabayashi, "'The Business of War': Google Employees Protest Work for the Pentagon," *New York Times*, April 4, 2018.

10. Primo Levi, *The Drowned and the Saved*, trans. Raymond Rosenthal (Summit Books, 1988), 38.

11. Levi, *The Drowned and the Saved*, 42.

12. Karl Marx, *Capital: A Critique of Political Economy*, vol. 1, trans. Ben Fowkes (Penguin Books, 1990), 873.

13. Marx, *Capital*, 917.

14. Marx, *Capital*, 925.

7. Marx and Darwin

1. Dominique Lecourt, "Marx in the Sieve of Darwin," trans. Erika Thomas, *Rethinking Marxism* 5, no. 4 (1992): 6.

2. For an explanation, see Lecourt, "Marx in the Sieve," 6–8. In the 1970s, two researchers (Margaret A. Fay and Lewis S. Feuer, working independently of one another) deduced that Darwin's October 13, 1880, letter was in fact addressed to Edward B. Aveling, in regard to Aveling's book *The Student's Darwin*—not to Marx in regard to *Capital*.

3. Lecourt, "Marx in the Sieve," 8.

4. Karl Marx, *Grundrisse: Foundations of the Critique of Political Economy (Rough Draft)*, trans. Martin Nicolaus (Penguin Books, 1973), 105.

5. Lecourt, "Marx in the Sieve," 26.

6. Lecourt, "Marx in the Sieve," 21.

7. Marx, *Capital*, 103.

8. Marc Andreessen, "The Techno-Optimist Manifesto," *Marc Andreessen Substack*, October 13, 2023, https://pmarca.substack.com/p/the-techno-optimist-manifesto.

9. Andreessen, "The Techno-Optimist Manifesto."

10. Andreessen, "The Techno-Optimist Manifesto."

8. Intelligent Extermination

1. Yuval Abraham, "'Lavender': The AI Machine Directing Israel's Bombing Spree in Gaza," *+972 Magazine*, April 3, 2024, https://www.972mag.com/lavender-ai-israeli-army-gaza/.

2. Abraham, "'Lavender.'" The book, self-published under the pseudonym "Brigadier General Y.S.," is titled *The Human-Machine Team: How to Create Synergy Between Human & Artificial Intelligence That Will Revolutionize Our World*. *+972*'s reporting identified the author as "the current commander of the elite Israeli intelligence unit 8200."

3. Abraham, "'Lavender.'"

4. See Yuval Noah Harari, *Homo Deus: A Brief History of Tomorrow* (Harper, 2017).

5. See Eyal Weizman, "Israel's New Commander in Chief: 'We'll Create a Deadlier Army!,'" interview by Marc Steiner, Real News Network, January 31, 2019, https://therealnews.com/israels-new-commander-in-chief-well-create-a-deadlier-army.

9. The Biblical Contagion

1. President Trump Leads a Cabinet Meeting at the White House, 08.26.25," Trump Transcripts, website of the Senate Democrats, September 26, 2025, https://www.democrats.senate.gov/newsroom/trump-transcripts/transcript-president-trump-leads-a-cabinet-meeting-at-the-white-house-082625.

2. Exod. 15:6 (New International Version).

3. Ps. 18:40–45 (NIV).

4. Shakespeare, *King Lear*, act 1, scene 5, line 45.

5. Ps. 127:3–5 (NIV).

10. Pater Noster

1. Lucretius, *The Nature of Things*, trans. Frank O. Copley (W. W. Norton, 1977), 2–3.

2. See Amin Maalouf, *The Crusades Through Arab Eyes*, trans. Jon Rothschild (Schocken Books, 1985).

3. See Samir Kassir, *Being Arab*, trans. Will Hobson (Verso, 2006).

4. Gen. 22:1–10 (NIV).

5. Søren Kierkegaard, *Fear and Trembling: A Dialectical Lyric*, trans. Walter Lowrie (Princeton University Press, 1945), 79–84.

6. Luke 22:42 (NIV).

7. Adolf von Harnack, *Marcion: The Gospel of the Alien God*, trans. John E. Steely and Lyle D. Bierma (Labyrinth, 1990), 3.

8. See Judith M. Lieu, *Marcion and the Making of a Heretic: God and Scripture in the Second Century* (Cambridge University Press, 2015).

9. Harnack, *Marcion*, 72.

10. Harnack, *Marcion*, 3.

11. Harnack, *Marcion*, 13.

12. Harnack, *Marcion*, 23.

13. Gal. 3:13, 5:1, 5:4 (NIV).

14. Gal. 3:28 (NIV).

15. Harnack, *Marcion*, 96.

9. Postface to the Second Italian Edition

1. "Humanity Will Shrink, Far Sooner Than You Think," *The Economist*, September 11, 2025.

2. See Kevin Kelly, *Out of Control: The Rise of Neo-Biological Civilization* (Basic Books, 1992).

3. See Alan Pifer and D. Lydia Bronte, "Squaring the Pyramid," introduction to "The Aging Society," ed. Stephen R. Graubard, *Daedalus: Journal of the American Academy of Arts and Sciences* 115, no. 1 (1986): 1–11.

4. See Alan Pifer and Lydia Bronte, eds., *Our Aging Society: Paradox and Promise* (W. W. Norton, 1986).

5. Marx, *Grundrisse*, 706.

ABOUT THE AUTHOR

Franco Berardi, aka "Bifo," founder of the famous Radio Alice in Bologna and an important figure of the Italian Autonomia movement, is a writer, philosopher, and media activist. He teaches at the Accademia di Brera, Milan.